THE GREAT MYSTERIES OF ARCHAEOLOGY

© 2007 E-ducation.it, Firenze
A SCALA Group company
www.e-ducation.it
info@e-ducation.it

This 2008 edition published
by Metro Books,
by arrangement with
E-ducation.it.

Project Director: Cinzia Caiazzo
Editor-in-chief: Filippo Melli
Texts: Renzo Rossi
Scientific Advice: Judith Lange
Editorial Staff: Giulia
Marrucchi, Sibilla Pierallini
Captions: Eva-Shaaron
Magrelli, Francesca Taddei
Graphics: Antonio Marchi
Translation: Russell Hall

Photographs:
© 2007 SCALA GROUP,
Firenze: © HIP; © Pierpont
Morgan Library / Art Resource;
© SCALA GROUP and COREL
All rights reserved; © S012-
Gamma Presse/Contrasto;
© Wolfgang Kaehler/Corbis;
© Roger Viollet/Alinari;
De Agostini: © G. Dagli Orti/
De Agostini, © G. Sioen/
De Agostini; © Griffith Institute,
University of Oxford; ©
Giovanni Caselli; © Gloria Rosati

Illustrations, selected from
the Scala Archives, of property
belonging to the Italian
Republic are published by
concession of the competent
authority (Ministero per i Beni
e le Attività Culturali).

Metro Books
122 Fifth Avenue
New York, NY 10011

ISBN-13: 978-1-4351-0740-3
ISBN-10: 1-4351-0740-3

Printed and bound in China

1 3 5 7 9 10 8 6 4 2

THE GREAT MYSTERIES OF ARCHAEOLOGY

TUTANKHAMUN

METRO BOOKS
NEW YORK

TABLE OF CONTENTS

Funeral mask
of Tutankhamun,
from the tomb
of the pharaoh,
c.1330 BC.
EgyptianMuseum,
Cairo. This mask,
of gold and
precious stones,
was placed
directly on the
mummy of the
king.

THE DISCOVERY

The god Anubis on a sedan chair in the form of a sacellum, from the tomb of Tutankhamun, c.1330 BC. Egyptian Museum, Cairo. Anubis, represented with the features of a jackal, was the divinity who accompanied the dead to the afterlife.

This statue of the god Anubis was found in the tomb of the young pharaoh Tutankhamun, who lived in Egypt 3,500 years ago and died when he was only 18 years old. The eternal sleep of this sovereign, an omnipotent living deity, was interrupted in 1922 by a genial English archaeologist called Howard Carter, who had been sifting the sands of the Valley of the Kings for 14 years in search of this burial place. The hypogeum of Tutankhamun, modest and anonymous on the outside, hid in its untouched rooms the richest treasures from ancient Egypt that had ever been seen: brilliant gold artefacts encrusted with precious materials. Scientists and archaeologists found themselves involved in the event of the century – it was a staggering discovery, filled with mystery, wonder and adventure and all eyes were fixed on Tutankhamun, a pharaoh who had been almost completely ignored by the ancient chroniclers.

The Reawakening of Tutankhamun

View of the Valley of the Kings, where the discovery of Carnarvon and Carter took place.

The story begins in the Valley of the Kings, a bare, parched landscape along the banks of the Nile, hiding, deep underground, the secret sepulchres of the pharaohs of the Eighteenth Dynasty.

In 1907, two men very different from one another – the aristocratic Lord Carnarvon, lover of the ancient world, and the professional archaeologist, Howard Carter – were brought together by a shared passion for Egyptology, and by a challenge: to find the tomb of Tutankhamun. A third man was involved, the American multimillionaire Theodore Davis, an amateur archaeologist obsessed with the idea of finding treasure of gold. Gaston Maspero, Director of the Egyptian Antiquities Service, gave them a license to dig in the Valley of the Kings; a site which was apparently without much interest, since it had been ransacked from the time of Giovanni Battista Belzoni.

However, Carnarvon and Carter were of a different

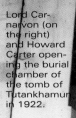

28

Lord Carnarvon (on the right) and Howard Carter opening the burial chamber of the tomb of Tutankhamun in 1922.

The Pyramid of Chefren; one of the monuments visited by Belzoni during his journey around Egypt, c. 2540 BC. Giza.

Giovanni Battista Belzoni

A native of Padua, Belzoni (1778-1823) was a circus performer, inventor, adventurer and a successful explorer in the pay of the English, who had few scruples when it came to stealing ancient artefacts. He was in Egypt for four years from 1815, exploring the principal archaeological sites. He was the first to enter the Great Temple at Abu Simbel, and discovered numerous tombs in the Valley of the Kings, including those of Ramses I and Seti I. At Giza he managed to enter the pyramid of Chefren and, in 1818, was the first person in modern times to see the sarcophagus of the pharaoh. Despite earning a reputation as a plunderer, Belzoni did attract the attention of scholars to the monuments of ancient Egypt, previously entirely hidden, and his archaeological finds form the basis of the Egyptian collection in the British Museum.

The tomb of Tutankhamun (H) in the Valley of the Kings, at the time of the excavations.

view, even though their hope of finding a tomb – especially that of Tutankhamun – was based on extremely slight archaeological evidence: a ceramic cup with the name of the pharaoh, a broken wooden box with gold leaf outlining the same name, and terracotta vases containing linen bandages traceable to Tutankhamun's funeral

ceremony. Carter, Carnarvon and Davis began their search, with Carter's scientific rigour often making his companions impatient. Davis was the first to give up, after seven years of digging. Lord Carnarvon renewed the licence until 1923, but he too lost faith in the enterprise and returned to England at the outbreak of the First World War.

The Certainty of Carter

Carter did not abandon the search. He was certain that all the tombs of the Eighteenth Dynasty were to be found in the valley, including the sepulchre of Tutankhamun – the pharaoh who had restored the worship of the god Amon, renounced by his father Akhenaten. A stele found at Karnak, on which it was written that Tutankhamun had been enthroned and that he had erected a golden statue to the god Amon when the country was 'invaded by evil', served to support Carter's thesis. His archaeologist's sound instinct, as well as six years of tenacious searching, led him to concentrate work in the area around the base of the tomb of Ramses VI.

He methodically subdivided the terrain into rectangles, marking every completed excavation with an 'X'. On 4th November, 1922, just one 'X' was missing from the map when a step emerged from the sand. Carter removed more sand and the step quickly became 16, stopping in front of a door. Behind this door was a corridor blocked with rubble, leading to a second door. Rather than immediately embarking upon the excavation, Carter cabled Carnarvon in England: 'At last have made wonderful discovery in Valley / a magnificent tomb with seals intact / recovered same for your arrival / Congratulations'.

For two weeks Carter resisted the desire to open the tomb, protecting it with an armed guard, because one thing was certain: the

Wooden statue from the tomb of Tutankhamun, c.1330 BC. Egyptian Museum, Cairo. The statue depicts the sovereign at rest, accompanied by the symbols of his power.

Howard Carter

In 1891, when he arrived in Cairo, Howard Carter was just 17 years old. A talented illustrator, he worked alongside the Egyptologist, William Flinders Petrie of the Egyptian Exploration Fund, during the excavations at Thebes. Spartan in his habits – he slept in a tent while Carnarvon stayed in luxurious hotels – Carter lived for archaeology. At the age of 25 he was nominated Superintendent of the Monuments of Upper Egypt – that is, those at Karnak, Luxor and in the Valley of the Kings. Supported by the American benefactor and amateur archaeologist, Theodore Davis, Carter discovered the tomb of Thutmosis IV but his involvement in a fight – which had serious repercussions for the colonial authorities – led to Carter being dismissed, and he was reduced to selling watercolours to tourists at the Winter Palace in Luxor. It was here, in 1907, that he met Lord Carnarvon. From that moment he had just one thought: to find the tomb of Tutankhamun.

When the great discovery came about it was after years of exhausting search, in the face of experts who had sifted the valley floor and declared that no strip remained unexplored.

Remaining in Cairo, Carter spent ten years cataloguing the objects accompanying Tutankhamun to the afterlife, and then went on to inspect the mummy. Ill and exhausted, he died at the age of 66, having resisted taking part in the explosion of media interest in his discovery.

sepulchre had not been violated. Twenty days later, Lord Carnarvon arrived in Luxor with his daughter, Lady Evelyn. The English nobleman was impatient and excited, but Carter maintained his habitual calm and, after freeing the corridor of its rubble, discovered on the second door not only the seal of the pharaoh, Tutankhamun, but also the seals of priests, evidence that an attempted robbery had been thwarted in ancient times.

View of the tomb of Ramses VI in the Valley of the Kings, near where the tomb of Tutankhamun was discovered.

'I can see marvellous things...'

Statue of Tutankhamun, from the tomb of Tutankhamun, c.1330 BC. Egyptian Museum, Cairo. This statue, like its counterpart, represents *ka* (the soul, the double spirit) of the pharaoh.

Carter made an opening, just large enough to poke his head through, in the left corner, and placed a candle in the hole. What he saw left him flabbergasted: 'I can see marvellous things', he exclaimed. It was the antechamber to the tomb, filled with statues, decorations, artefacts and gold: gold everywhere. Before his eyes was the realisation of every archaeologist's dream and they had to extract him from that window of marvels 'like a cork from a bottle'.

On 27th November, when the door was finally opened, Lord Carnarvon, his daughter and the Egyptologist, Callender, who had arrived as soon as he heard the news of the discovery, could also see, in the light thrown by a powerful electric lamp, the sparkling of precious chests, a golden throne, alabaster vases, bizarre animal heads serving as sentinels, and, one in front of the other, two statues with aprons and golden sandals. But nowhere amongst all this treasure was there a sarcophagus or a mummy.

The discovery of a third door, which showed signs of break-in and re-sealing, led to renewed hope, although they failed to understand why thieves should have endeavoured to penetrate the third door without first carrying away the precious objects from the preceding room.

And the surprises were not yet over. There was a small lateral room, crammed with archaeological treasures of every type, removed and partially damaged by unknown visitors.

Lord Carnarvon

The extremely rich young aristocratic, Lord Carnarvon, was a sportsman, art collector, horse lover and motorcar fanatic. Following a serious car accident, he decided – as was the habit of convalescing aristocrats – to winter somewhere with a hot climate and his choice fell upon Luxor in the 'Land of the Pharaohs'. This was where his interest in archaeology began.

Despite having no experience, he obtained a licence in 1907 to dig in the Valley of the Kings from the Director of the Egyptian Antiquities Service, Maspero, who teamed him up with a young archaeologist, Howard Carter. The Valley of Kings appeared to have little more to offer as far as excavations were concerned, and their finds were few – though important: the tomb of Amenhotep I, and a stele that recounted, in epic form, the Kahmose's war of liberation of against the Hyksos.

Disheartened, Carnarvon often returned to England for lengthy periods, limiting his activity to financing Carter's enterprises. On hearing the news of the discovery of the tomb of Tutankhamun, he rushed back to Egypt to witness the opening of the tomb. He missed the opening of the Tutankhamun sarcophagus in 1924, however, having died of an insect bite.

Dignitaries visiting the tomb of Tutankhamun at the time of the excavations. Valley of the Kings.

Workers inside the antechamber of the tomb of Tutankhamun, packing up one of the two statues of the pharaoh, which guarded the burial chamber.

Tutankhamun: a Scoop

Throne of Tutankhamun, from the tomb of Tutankhamun, c.1330 BC. Egyptian Museum, Cairo. From the antechamber of the tomb; covered in gold leaf and ornamented with precious stones.

Stunned by the worldwide clamour following the finding of the Tutankhamun sepulchre and irritated by the arrival of thousands of photographers, tourists and government officials, Carter decided to interrupt excavations in February 1923. But the flow of visitors was not halted. Thanks to the rapid diffusion of photographic reporting all over the world Tutankhamun had become the focus of a mass media cult.

The quantity of unearthed material was enormous and the immense task of its classification, cataloguing, removal and conservation had yet to be embarked upon. After consulting with the specialists – photographers, artists, chemists, historians, engineers and botanists – who had arrived from American and European universities and museums, the first object was brought to the surface on 27th December, and this removal work went on for almost two months. The antechamber alone contained around 700 pieces, and it took entire weeks to empty some single casks of their contents.

In addition, there were three bulky coffins, a throne with its decorated backrest, and four carriages which, given their size, had not been introduced into the tomb in one piece but sawn into various sections, which thieves had subsequently scattered about.

Opposite: Throne of Tutankhamun, detail of the back with the pharaoh and the queen depicted under a solar disc, from the tomb of Tutankhamun, c.1330 BC. Egyptian Museum, Cairo.

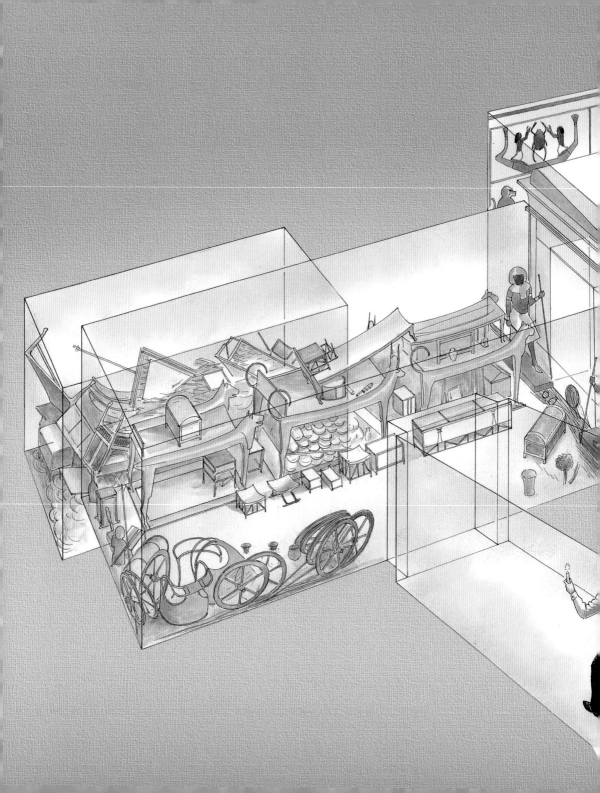

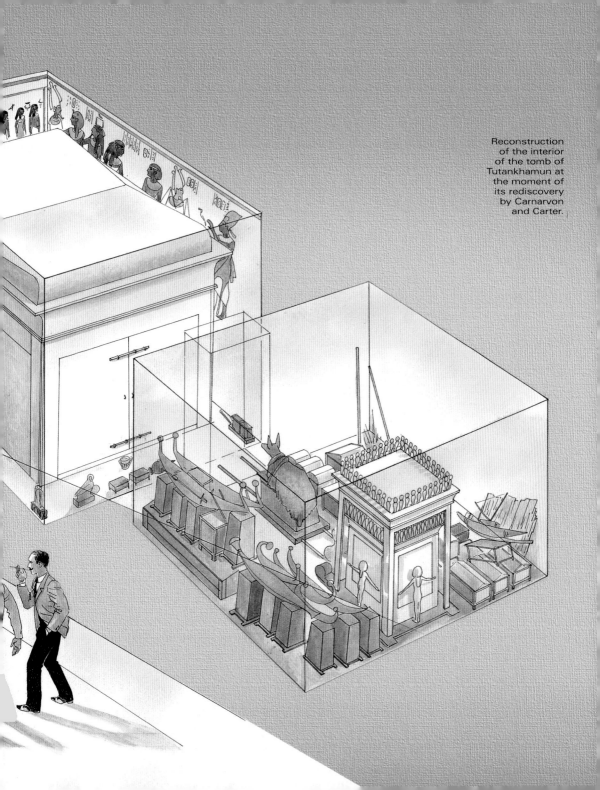

Reconstruction of the interior of the tomb of Tutankhamun at the moment of its rediscovery by Carnarvon and Carter.

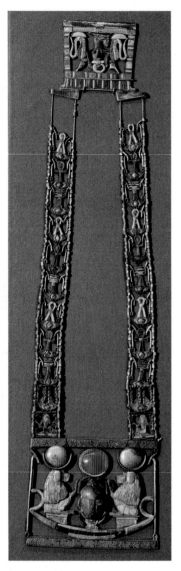

Large necklace and breastplate, from the tomb of Tutankhamun, c.1330 BC. Depicted on the necklace are symbols and divinities in the form of a cobra, a baboon and a scarab beetle.

The Burial Chamber

By mid-February, 1923, the antechamber had been cleared, and it was time to move on to the opening of the door, which, it was hoped, hid the mummy.

On 17th February, twenty people – members of the government and scientists – were admitted to the interior of the tomb to observe the great event. In absolute silence, Carter began to remove the upper layer of stone. As soon as the opening became large enough to allow an electric lamp to pass through, a marvellous vision appeared. It was a wall of solid gold, which turned out to be the anterior wall of the largest funerary coffin that has ever been discovered. After two hours of difficult work, they penetrated the interior of the burial chamber where a catafalque, completely covered with gold, its sides inlaid with panels of azure majolica and

covered with symbols, was revealed. Its dimensions left the observers stunned: 5.20m x 3.35m x 2.75m.

On 29th November, 1923, work began on taking apart the catafalque, which consisted of four coffins placed one inside the other. The large, unsealed double doors on the western side opened easily, but the second coffin – which lay inside – still bore a seal: it was intact, and Tutankhamun rested in his tomb just as he had when placed there 33 centuries earlier. The emotion felt by those present was so profound that the adjacent treasure chamber, which also contained artefacts of incalculable value, passed almost unobserved.

The task of removal took 84 days, at the end of which the explorers found themselves in front of the enormous sarcophagus, carved from a single block of yellow quartz and covered with a

With the aid of a mechanical device to help lift the heavy lid, Carnarvon and Carter open the sarcophagus that enclosed the mummy of Tutankhamun.

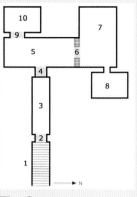

The Structure of the Tomb

Smaller and more modest than all the other tombs in the Valley of the Kings, Tutankhamun's would appear to have been a makeshift affair, perhaps as a result of the pharaoh's sudden and unexpected death. Sixteen descending steps (1) lead to the first sealed door (2), from which parts a 17-metre long corridor (3), which terminates at a second sealed door (4). The rectangular antechamber is entered from here (5), this being equipped with two further sealed doors. The right-hand door of the antechamber (6) opens into the burial chamber, decorated with wall paintings, in which was placed the golden treasure chest and the niche containing the pharaoh's sarcophagus (7). The room forming an annexe to the burial chamber (8) was reserved for further treasures. The fourth sealed door (9) separated the antechamber from a walled room (10) and contained yet more treasure.

granite slab. The opening of the sarcophagus took place on the 12th February, 1924. Under linen bandages appeared the king: not the mummy but a portrait in gold of the young pharaoh.

The completely rounded head had its face painted with gold, the eyes with aragonite and obsidian, and the eyelashes and eyebrows with lapis lazuli. The hands were fully formed, whilst the body was in *bas-relief*.

Carnavon's death and squabbles with the authorities interrupted further investigation and it was only in 1925 that Carter could get back to work and, removing the last casings, finally get to the mummy of the pharaoh.

Gorget decorated with the vulture god, Nekhbet, from the tomb of Tutankhamun, c.1330 BC. Egyptian Museum, Cairo. This neck ornament, created for the pharaoh, depicts the god associated with Upper Egypt.

Opposite:
The chamber
housing the
sarcophagus
in the tomb of
Tutankhamun.
The back wall
depicts the
pharaoh in the
presence of the
gods.

Detail of the
sarcophagus of
Tutankhamun,
from the tomb
of Tutankha-
mun, c.1330
BC. Egyptian
Museum, Cairo.
This is the third
anthropoid
sarcophagus,
which lay inside
the great quartz
sarcophagus. It
contained the
mummy with its
funeral mask.

Floral funeral
collar, from
the tomb of
Tutankhamun,
c.1330 BC. Egyp-
tian Museum,
Cairo.

Ritual bed, from
the tomb of
Tutankhamun,
c.1330 BC. Egyp-
tian Museum,
Cairo. Along
with two similar
pieces of furni-
ture, this object
was found in
the antecham-
ber of the tomb.
The sides of the
bed are shaped
into the form
of a cow with
the solar disc
between its
horns.

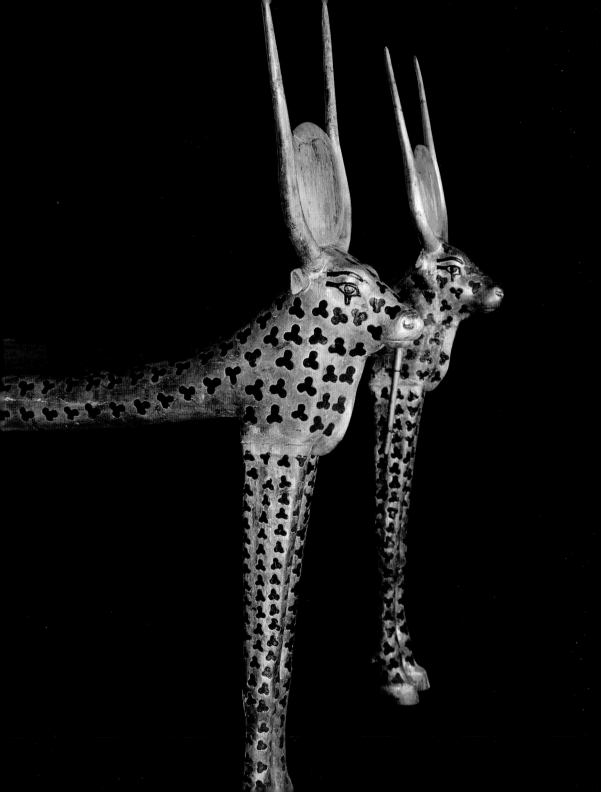

The Mummy
is Brought to Light

Carter in 1925, during work to remove encrustations of resins and bitumen from the third sarcophagus of Tutankhamun.

This was the last task carried out before arriving at the mummy of the pharaoh.

When the mummy of Tutankhamun appeared before the experts, it soon became evident that the oils and resins that had been used in its preparation had hardened and glued everything together. With the exception of the face, feet and hands, which were encased in gold, the oxidisation of resin compounds had almost completely carbonised the body tissues and bones.

The medical-biological examination revealed that the pharaoh was about 1.65 metres tall, slight in build and with an extremely elongated head. An X-ray of the mummy carried out in 1968 by a professor of anatomy revealed that there was a serious injury on the left cheekbone, of unknown origin. Using the funeral mask and cranium as a base there has been a laboratory reconstruction of the face of Tutankhamun: he appears to have been a handsome young man, resembling images of his father, Amenhotep IV-Akhenaten.

The Final Destination: Cairo

The lid of a Canopus vase, from the tomb of Tutankhamun, c.1330 BC. Egyptian Museum, Cairo. These vases were designed to contain the organs of the deceased, which were removed during the preparation of the mummy.

From the start, envy and squabbling accompanied the discovery and exploration of Tutankhamun's tomb and Carter had to battle not to lose the right to examine his 'creature', being undermined by European and American Egyptologists. Ownership was also questioned, with Cairo laying claim to the 'booty' by citing a clause in the licence to excavate which gave Egypt the right to all archaeological treasures found, should the tomb 'not have been visited by thieves'.

Attempts at theft had been made, albeit unsuccessfully, and Carnarvon's heirs used this clause to attempt to take the treasure to Britain; but Carter, the true instigator of the discovery, signed a document in which he gave up any claim to the finds, which consequently remained in Egypt. They can still be seen today, in the Cairo Museum.

Headrest, from
the tomb of
Tutankhamun,
c.1330 BC.
Egyptian
Museum, Cairo.
In the centre is
Shu; the divinity
usually depicted
supporting the
vault of heaven.

Vase in the form of a lion, from the tomb of Tutankhamun, c.1330 BC. Egyptian Museum, Cairo. These objects, generally of ivory, would have contained perfumed unguents.

Unguent vase, from the tomb of Tutankhamun, c. 1330 BC. Egyptian Museum, Cairo. The unusual form of the vase symbolises the unification of Upper and Lower Egypt.

Games table, from the tomb of Tutankhamun, c.1330 BC. Egyptian Museum, Cairo. Boards such as this were used to play *sene*, as depicted in wall paintings.

Casket with
ivory inlays,
from the
tomb of
Tutankhamun,
c.1330 BC.
Egyptian
Museum, Cairo.
Many objects
of this type
were found
in the tomb.
They were
designed to
contain fabrics,
small objects,
unguents and
cosmetics, to
accompany the
deceased to the
afterlife.

TUTANKHAMUN AND THE VALLEY OF THE KINGS

View of the
Valley of the
Kings, showing
the entrances to
several tombs.

Tutankhamun and the pharaohs of the New Kingdom had themselves buried in the Valley of the Kings (Biban el-Muluk): an arid, rocky depression lying alongside the eastern bank of the Nile, facing Karnak and Luxor and overlooked by a mountain called Qurn ('Horn'), the highest summit in the valley, and immediately recognisable by its pyramid-like shape, which was probably significant for the ancient Egyptians. The area comprises the eastern valley – the most important, in which 58 tombs have been discovered – and a branch leading off it, the western valley, with four tombs.

Up until the decline of the Twentieth Dynasty, the pharaohs generally chose long tunnels, sometimes penetrating deep into the mountain, for their burials. The entrances could be hidden, perhaps with stones, although some were more visible: inspections took place – these being well documented – and there was precise data on their location. The internal structure of the tombs reveals three phases of elaboration, roughly corresponding to the three dynasties of the New Kingdom (Eighteenth, Nineteenth, Twentieth). During the

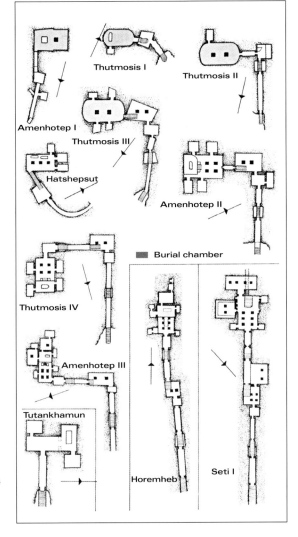

Thutmosis I

Thutmosis II

Amenhotep I

Thutmosis III

Hatshepsut

Amenhotep II

■ Burial chamber

Thutmosis IV

Amenhotep III

Tutankhamun

Horemheb

Seti I

Evolution in the design of tombs during the New Kingdom, Six-teenth-Twelfth centuries BC.

Eighteenth Dynasty, the tombs were planned with a clear bending or curving of their axes. With Horemheb, the last king of the Eighteenth Dynasty, there is a change. The plan becomes straighter, but the corridor is 'split', continuing in parallel, with a 'bayonet-like' junction. During the Twentieth Dynasty, the plan tended to become simpler and was straight again. These were not showy sepulchres, attractive prey for robbers, but underground passages for the corpse of the pharaoh to lie in forever. Nevertheless, the majority of these tombs were ransacked in ancient times.

During the New Kingdom, the tombs were no longer considered places of worship and great funeral temples, such as those of Queen Hatshepsut (Eighteenth Dynasty) and the Ramesseum of Ramses II (Nineteenth Dynasty), were constructed at other sites. In order to maintain secrecy, the workers were not housed in the immediate vicinity of the burial place, but some distance away at Deir el-Medina.

The Valley of the Queens

Southeast of the Valley of the Kings, another valley opens out at the foot of a kind of open-air cave, recognisable from a distance by overhanging rocks, which appear about to tumble down.

From time to time, rainwater forms a waterfall and collects in a basin. Perhaps because this suggested a female symbol, the valley was chosen as the 'Seat of Beauty', nowadays known as the Valley of the Queens: a necropolis for queens and royal princes and princesses, especially of the Nineteenth and Twentieth Dynasties.

These tombs are similar to those of the pharaohs, but are simpler in their design, and decorated in a different manner, with images featuring the dead in front of the gods. That of the bride of Ramses II, Nefertari, has intensely contrasting chromatic scenes, and the tombs of two of the children of Ramses III are particularly notable for their bright colours. At the edge of the desert, following the cultivated land, there are the remains of temples of worship – 'castles of millions of years' – corresponding to royal burial places.

Necropolis
of the Valley
of the Queens.

The Workers
of Deir el-Medina

The village of Deir el-Medina, where the workers and artists that worked on the tombs of the Valley of the Kings lived, grew up in a narrow, isolated, waterless valley, to the west of Luxor, at the foot of the mountain where the sepulchres of the New Kingdom were dug.

Since the secret of the burials had to be well kept, the community was kept under tight surveillance, being supplied with everything it required, but effectively segregated. The village, which was surrounded by a wall of bricks and mud with a single entrance, was home to up to 1000 inhabitants, not all of whom worked at the necropolis. Alongside the manual workers, navvies, foremen, architects, sculptors and painters were the scribes who had the task of organising the work, and the managers of the warehouses, which were full of building materials (coloured pigments, copper tools, wood for scaffolding). There were also those who provided public services, such as water bearers, people tending animals and the women who cultivated wheat to make bread and barley for beer.

All other consumer goods, above all salt, were brought in from outside and constituted

Model of a procession of porters. Egyptian Museum, Cairo. Objects such as this enable us to reconstruct daily life in ancient times.

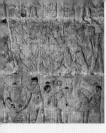

Bas-relief showing artisans at work, c. 2450 BC. Mastaba of Niankhnum and Khnumhotep, Saqqara.

Developments in the Work of Craftsmen

The conditions experienced by craftsmen during the New Kingdom changed considerably. They formed a 'middle class', well-integrated into the economic life of the country, although many of them – carpenters, sculptors, painters, metal workers – were employed by the court or temple. There was also development in the working practices of certain craftsmen, as contact with the peoples annexed by the Empire enabled Egypt to get to know new materials and new techniques.

This was the case with iron, acquired from the Hittites during the campaign of Thutmosis III and his successors, and with glass, originating in Phoenicia, and arriving in Egypt halfway through the second millennium BC.

the wages of the workers. Aware of their importance as the builders of eternal resting places, the workers of Deir el-Medina knew how to protect their rights and, in extreme situations, even went on strike.

Before being abandoned and forgotten beneath the desert sands, Deir el-Medina was active for about 500 years.

In the tombs of the necropolis alongside the workers' village, religious themes dominate.

They are tombs of a modest

size, decorated by artists of proven ability, who had been trained to realise the most demanding commissions. Decoration is concentrated in the underground chambers, where it is more likely to have been preserved. A yellow background is common, throwing the scenes into relief. These were created with great skill, although without the inventiveness that can be seen in the tombs of the upper classes of the New Kingdom.

Stele from Deir-el
Medina, Thir-
teenth century BC.
British Museum
London.
The inscription in-
forms us that the
stele belonged to
the foreman
Qeh, one of
the workers
from the com-
munity of Deir
el-Medina.

The Search for Immortality

In the most ancient temples, it is clear that life after death was considered the privilege of the pharaohs. Their subjects hoped the immortality of the king would somehow reflect on them. By the end of the Old Kingdom, however, survival became a right for anyone who could possess a tomb and afford the funeral rites. Both the sacred tale of the death and rebirth of Osiris, and the daily fate of the Sun god – shrouded in darkness at dusk, but rising triumphantly the following day – represented a guarantee that the soul survived after death. But for this to come about, the soul needed a body, which would not decay, or the soul would be condemned to passing eternity in the vain search for its physical embodiment. There arose the need to preserve the corpse via mummification, various burial practices, and substantial tombs.

Painted scene from *The Book of the Dead*, c.1420 BC. Egyptian Museum, Turin.

Ka-statue of King Anib-ra Hor, from Dahshur, Thirteenth Dynasty (1773-1650 BC). Egyptian Museum, Cairo. The double spirit of the king, his *ka*, is represented by a human figure surmounted by two raised arms.

The Survival of the Soul

The Egyptians believed that human life consisted of diverse elements, the survival of which would ensure immortality. The *ka* (represented by a pair of raised arms on a human figure) was a double spirit, created on a lathe at the moment of the birth of Khnum, the god of creation, and physically similar to its owner. During a person's life, the *ka* could leave the body during sleep, thereby causing damage to its owner.

At the moment of death, it would abandon the corpse and journey to the underground world in order to encounter Osiris, the god of the dead, and be judged. Each morning it would return to the land of the living, recognising the tomb of its owner from its pictures, statues and mummy. Here it received funeral offerings of food and drink from the priest.

The impersonal vital force

Painted scene from *The Book of the Dead*, c.1420 BC. Egyptian Museum, Turin. Detail of the god Osiris.

The Myth of Osiris

The myth of Osiris contrasts the fertility of the river-washed lands of the Nile with the aridity of the desert. Osiris is also, however, the king of the underworld, who offers a new form of existence to the souls of the deceased.

Osiris was at one time King of Egypt, betrothed to his sister Isis. Their evil brother, Set, who had married another sister, Nephthys, killed Osiris, tricking him into climbing into a sarcophagus, which was then abandoned to the currents of the Nile. Whilst Set ascended to the throne, Isis recovered the body of her husband at Biblo and took him back to Egypt. However, Set took possession of the corpse once again, cutting it into 14 pieces, which he scattered all over Egypt. Isis began a pilgrimage around the country and in all the places in which she found a piece of her husband's body places, she established a temple. This was the origin of the temples dedicated to Osiris at Abido (the Osireion), Busiri, Biga and elsewhere.

Having gathered all the pieces, Isis changed into a kite and, by twirling and screeching and provoking the wind with her wings, caused Osiris to return to life. This is the reason why many sarcophagi are decorated with the protective wings of Isis, to help infuse new life into the soul of the deceased.

With her resurrected husband, Isis conceived a son, Horus. Osiris became King of the Land of the Dead, whilst Horus was brought up by his mother so that he would avenge his father's murder. After years of battle with Set, Horus emerged the winner and became King of Egypt. In his honour, every successive king was considered the personification of Horus, from whom they had inherited the throne.

of man was known as the *ba*; this being symbolised by a bird with a human head, which could have either arms or wings. The *ba* abandoned the cadaver at the moment of death, becoming free to leave the tomb and then return, perching on the corpse.

The body was therefore necessary for the *ka* in order to find its way home, and for the *ba* as a perching place. The eternal survival of both depended, above all, on the conservation of the corpse.

Mummy of a baby with its painted portrait, from the Roman era, c.mid-first century BC. British Museum, London. The outer casing is meticulously decorated with various figurative scenes, the bandages of this type of mummy are wrapped to form a pattern of lozenges or diamonds.

The History of Mummification

The first conservation of human remains in Egypt must have come about by accident.

In the cemeteries of the Pre-Dynastic Era, made up of shallow ditches in which the dead were placed in a foetal position. The extremely hot, dry climate caused the corpses to desiccate naturally.

When dead bodies began to be placed in tombs with a lid, they were first wrapped in linen bandages then covered with compressed and polished chalk, so that they might take the form of the underlying corpse. Once the chalk had dried, the outer shell would be painted (often green, the colour of rebirth) and the face would be given the features of the deceased.

During the Middle Kingdom period, the techniques of mummification became more sophisticated, the best and definitive examples being from the time of the New Kingdom. In later eras there were

The *Moumiya*

The term 'mummy' would seem to derive from the Persian-Arabic word *moumiya*, which means 'bitumen' or 'pitch'; referring to the hard, black, resinous substance (a compound of oils, perfumes, unguents and resins) with which the Egyptians covered bodies in order to conserve them.

In the Middle Ages, Arab doctors considered the substances used in mummification to be potent medicaments. Egyptian mummies were therefore removed and their tissues reduced to powder and sold for medicinal purposes.

attempts to restore the corpse to its natural shape, with padding in linen and other materials, but the decay of these supports caused precisely the effects, which the embalmers were seeking to avoid. Once Christianity spread to Egypt, mummification was gradually abandoned.

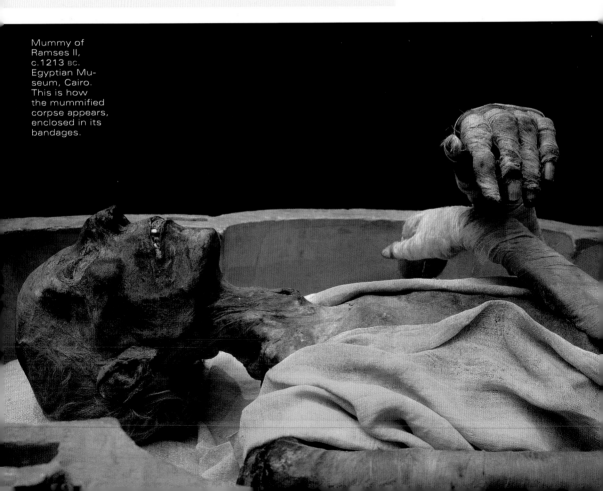

Mummy of Ramses II, c.1213 BC. Egyptian Museum, Cairo. This is how the mummified corpse appears, enclosed in its bandages.

The Process of Mummification

Herodotus described three different methods of mummification, each with a different price: simple washing and purification; the injection of corrosive liquids; and the incision and extraction of organs. The latter was the most expensive because it required the extraction of the intestines, stomach, liver and lungs through an abdominal incision. The kidneys – often considered the seat of the emotions – and the heart – which was necessary for the deceased in order to be judged – would be placed back inside the emptied corpse.

The brain was also removed, via an incision cut into the skull or through the nostrils, using hooks, and replaced by a metal skullcap. The internal organs were embalmed like the body and wrapped separately in bandages.

The body was then placed under piles of dried natron, a mineral salt that was abundantly available from the bed of a dried-out lake in the Eastern Delta (known nowadays as Wadi el-Natrun). It is largely composed of sodium chloride but contains a high percentage (17%) of sodium bicarbonate, indispensable for the procedure to be successful.

The natron absorbed the fluids of the body, which, after about 40 days (Herodotus says 70 days), became a solid shell, no longer subject to decomposition.

Linen bag containing salt used in the mummification process, New Kingdom (1550-1069 BC). British Museum, London.

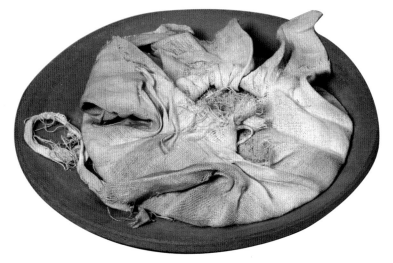

Canopic Vases

In the most ancient times, the internal organs extracted from the corpse were placed in a casket, internally divided into four parts, with lids in the form of human heads. Later, Canopic vases, retaining the four heads, came into use. In the era of the Ramses, these stood for the four children of Horus. Duamutef, with a jackal's head, contained the stomach; Kebechsenef, the falcon, conserved the intestines; the liver was placed in a vase with Imset's human head; and Hapi, with the head of a baboon, contained the lungs. The Canopic vases were often made of calcite and were placed in the tomb inside a chest.

Canopic vases, from the tomb of Tutankhamun, c.1330 BC. Egyptian Museum, Cairo. These vases were designed to contain the organs of the deceased, which were removed during the preparation of the mummy.

The Bandages

When the mummy was ready, it would be purified and the priests would proceed to the bandaging. Linen bandages were used, generally those available for household use.

Only for pharaohs, their families and other high dignitaries would specially woven bandages be utilised. First, the limbs would be bandaged, and then the rest of the body. The arms were wrapped around the body, and the legs bound together.

As the various layers of linen were being wound, amulets would be paced at fixed points and the priests recited prayers to ensure the success of the operation.

Often, upon completing the bandaging, a mask was placed over the face of the deceased; of gold or silver for a king; of painted papier-mâché (papyrus and linen mixed with chalk) for the less well off. The mummy was then placed in a painted, anthropoid coffin, which might be encased in further coffins. For the upper classes and the King, a rectangular stone sarcophagus was used.

During the bandaging, laying in the coffin and burial, great quantities of precious unguents and perfumes were poured, which would subsequently form the characteristic hard substance similar to pitch.

Linen bandages from the mummy of Djedher, from Saqqara, Fourth century BC. British Museum, London. Many of the bindings used to wrap the dead were covered in long, painted inscriptions like this.

Funeral mask
of Thuya,
from Thebes,
c.1360 BC.
Egyptian
Museum, Cairo.
These masks
were placed
on the face of
the deceased
immediately
after bandaging
was completed.

The Funeral Ceremony

The mummy in its coffin, with a canopy overhead representing the sky and the stars, was transported on a sledge towards the tomb. It was followed by a procession of people bearing food and drink, furniture and personal objects to decorate the burial chamber, accompanied by the funeral laments of the women.

At the entrance to the tomb, a ceremony known as the 'opening of the mouth' took place. The coffin would be raised vertically, so that a priest could delicately touch, with a miniature carpenter's axe, the points corresponding to the eyes, nose, lips, ears, hands and feet, as if to raise the wood and allow the senses to function. The ritual chant was: *'My mouth is open! My mouth is cleft by Shu [god of the air] with that metal lance which he used to open the mouths of the gods. I am the Powerful. I will sit next to he who is in the great breathing of the sky'* (*Book of the Dead*, Utterance 23).

The coffin was then lowered into the tomb and all the funeral objects placed around it. At this point the entrance would be sealed with mud and stones. In the western hills, an oval would be carved, with Anubis lying on nine bound prisoners. Between the stones, terracotta cones with the names and titles of the deceased might be inserted.

Sarcophagus lid, and detail. Musée du Louvre, Paris. Sarcophagi, designed to contain the mummy, were often richly decorated with figurative scenes, accompanied by inscriptions.

Analyses
of the Mummies

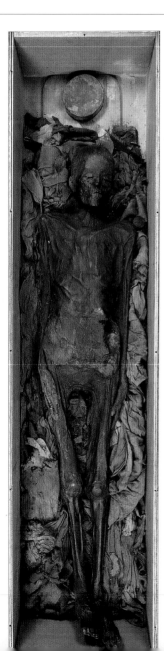

The number of mummies still extant is relatively small; it is calculated that there are just 1,000. Modern techniques allow for their examination without even removing their bandages but, up until the end of the Nineteenth century, the mummies would be unbandaged, and in many collections 'unwrapped' mummies are on display. Scientists have been able to obtain valuable information from these.

X-ray examinations have revealed various diseases, such as arthritis and gout, as well as fractures preceding or following death. Electronic microscopes have revealed particles of sand and carbon in the lungs – Egypt is windy and sandy – and infestations of parasites, including bilharzia,

which is still widespread today. This is a tiny worm, which enters the body through the skin of the feet and attacks organs, including the lungs and optic nerves, in the latter case causing immediate and irreversible blindness. Almost all the mummies show signs of serious damage to their teeth; not caused by caries, but by the wearing away of tooth enamel down to the dentin, caused by the sand present in food, particularly bread. One surprise is the recent discovery that DNA is still intact in the cells of mummified tissues.

Paradoxically, if the mummies were ever to be cloned, the ancient Egyptians would have succeeded in their aim: 'to live forever'.

Mummy
of a woman,
c. 600 BC.
British Museum,
London.

Utterances for the Beyond

The belief that assistance and protection must be provided for the dead in their afterlife dates back to very ancient times. Already by the Pre-Dynastic Era, there was provision of food, drink and rush matting in even the humblest tombs.

The earliest inscriptions to refer to an afterlife were found in the burial chambers of pyramids that date back to the Fifth and Sixth Dynasties. These are known as the *Pyramid Texts.*

At the end of the Ancient Kingdom, during the Twelfth Dynasty, people of high status, as well as the pharaoh, were given their own tombs. The 'utterances' were written on the interior of the coffin.

Funerary figurines called ushabti were also placed in the tombs, to relieve the deceased of his daily toils and serve the gods in his name. Then, during the New Kingdom, magical expressions written on papyrus scrolls, known as *Texts of the Sarcophagi*, were put in tombs, and, from the Eighteenth Dynasty, large, hollow wooden statues, shaped like the mummy, contained the papyrus scroll known as *The Book of the Dead.*

Box with *ushabti*, from the tomb of Henutmehyt, c.1250 BC. British Museum, London. These statuettes were designed to carry out everyday tasks for the deceased in the afterlife.

The *Pyramid Texts*

The documents known as the *Pyramid Texts* are not, as is often claimed, a complex of texts, but rather a total of 759 'spells' or utterances, which do not appear in their entirety in any one pyramid. They were probably recited ('uttered') as the body of the king was being prepared for burial, while the mummy was laid in its sarcophagus and when the funeral objects were carried into the tomb. Their language suggests that they come from an extremely ancient tradition but the first to be engraved were those found in the pyramid of Unas, who reigned at the end of the Fifth Dynasty, towards 2490 BC. Utterance 554 describes the pharaoh as a 'Powerful Bull', which takes its place with the gods among the stars: 'You are the son of the Great White Cow! She conceived you, she gave birth to you and she protects you.

She will cross the river with you, since you are at one with those who stay around the Sun and surround the Morning Star!' In their company, the King would also become a star: 'The sky is limpid and Sothis shines because I, son of Sothis, am alive and the gods have purified themselves for me in the Great Bear, the imperishable stars' (Utterance 302). The final group of utterances, which date back to the Ancient Kingdom, show the king linked to Ra, the lord of the Sun. This was probably due to the proclamation of Ra as national divinity during the Fifth Dynasty.

From that moment it was believed that the destiny of the king was to sail every day with the Sun god in his boat across the heavens.

Wall with images of gods in relief, Fourth century BC. Temple of Horus, Edfu.

The scenes are accompanied by inscriptions invoking gods and the pharaoh.

The *Texts of the Sarcophagi*

The *Texts of the Sarcophagi*, which began to appear with the onset of the Middle Kingdom, offered protection against eternal hunger, thirst and the terrible heat of the sun, as well as speaking for the first time of the perilous journey the soul has to undertake in order to reach the land where he can live for eternity. A map of the underground world would be added. The *Texts of the Sarcophagi* are much more difficult to understand than the *Texts of the Pyramids*; they communicate a sense of fearful anticipation for the ordeals the soul will have to undergo on its journey: 'Do not fear for my body, for words and magic defeat evil on my behalf. I will see the Lord of Light, and I will live there.

Let me pass! Show me Num and Amon! They do not dare to speak, for they are afraid of he whose name is hidden in my body. I know him! I have everything that is required to pass through his door!'

Sarcophagus of the priest Hor, with inscriptions, from Deir el-Bahari, 680 BC. British Museum, London

The *Book of the Dead*

The papyri that make up *The Book of the Dead* are usually written in hieroglyphics, and the most beautiful are also magnificently illustrated. The length of the papyri varies from a few centimetres to 23 metres. In total they contain about 200 spells or instructions, though no two papyri have exactly the same texts. Each book begins with the spell that the priests recited in the presence of the deceased's mummy, whilst they inserted amulets between the bandages to act as protection.

After the ceremony of the 'opening of the mouth', the soul had to leave the body and confront demons, who often assumed the form of reptiles or crocodiles armed with sharp knives, but who could be kept at bay with this threat: 'Back! Get away from me, evil one! Do not force me to utter your name to the god which sent you here [...] O you who speaks against this magic of mine, no crocodile that lives under a spell will carry me away!' (Utterance 23). The deceased would be judged by Osiris for his actions during his life; Horus would bring him before the god, who was assisted by Isis and Nephtys.

Magic formulae helped the soul overcome the trial. This also took place in the hall of justice, when Isis would remove the heart from the corpse, prior to offering it to Anubis while reciting more magic formulae. Anubis placed the heart on one of the plates of a set of scales, weighing it against the feather of Maat.

Thoth would wait, pen in hand, while the heart was being judged, ready to write down the sentence. The protection of the Book of the Dead would ensure that Osiris judged the soul to be 'of sincere voice', thereby allowing it to join its ancestors in the 'Land of Reeds'.

Following pages: *The Book of the Dead*. Ägyptisches Museum, Berlin. These papyri were deposited with the deceased and were intended to help the soul receive a positive judgement from the god Osiris.

Papyrus from *The Book of the Dead* of the scribe Nebqed, c.1300 BC. Musée du Louvre, Paris. The mummy of the deceased, laid out in a sacred boat, is being transported to the afterworld, while several porters bear gifts.

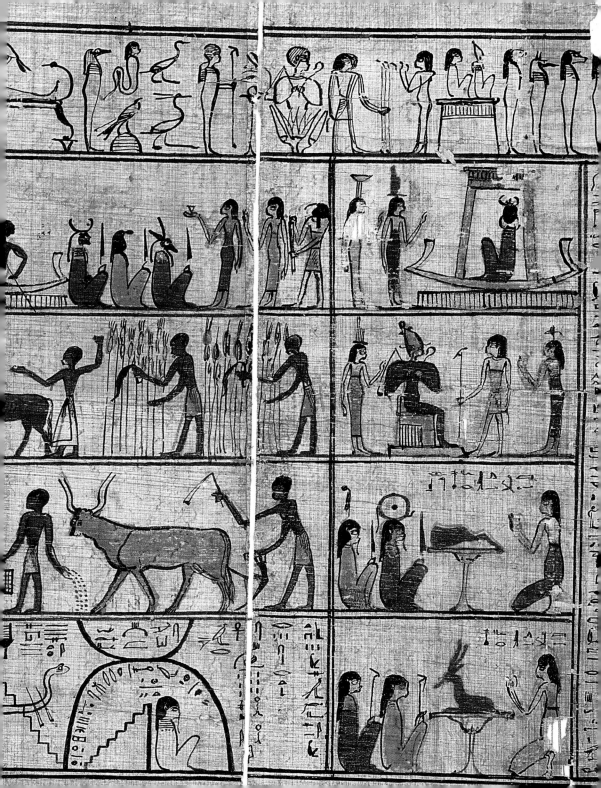

Detail from *The Book of the Dead* of Maiherperi, showing the weighing of the soul, from Thebes, c.1450 BC. Egyptian Museum, Cairo.

Without the assistance of the book it was probable that the heart would be judged guilty. In this case the soul of the deceased would be consumed by Amenti, a monstous spirit with the jaws of a crocodile - half leopard, half hippopotamus - and would thus die a second time, for eternity.

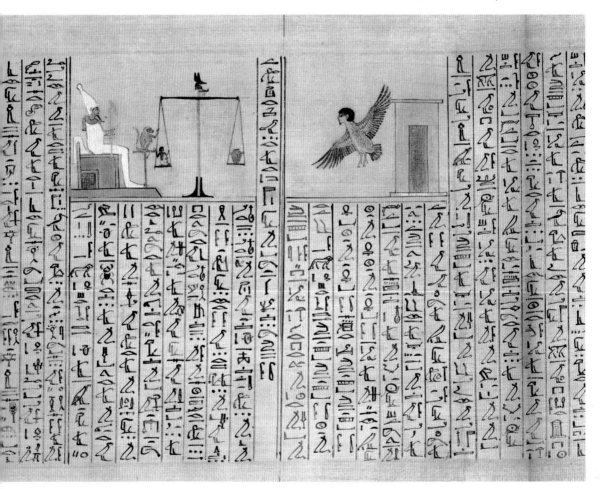

The *Ushabti*

The afterworld was viewed as an eternal and spiritual country, where the deceased feared he would have to work for the gods, as he had in this life for the pharaohs, in a system of enforced labour. During the Middle Kingdom, recourse was made to small figurines, in painted wood or limestone. When the god called the soul to his service, these 'workers' would respond on his behalf. The Egyptian word for 'response' is 'usheb', hence these figurines were called 'ushabti'.

They would be engraved with the name of the dead person, or with the following formula: 'Oh *ushabti*, if I am called upon to carry out some work in the land of the dead, if problems arise for me working in the fields, irrigating the land or while transporting stone on the boats, you will say: I will do it! You will respond: Here I am!' In one tomb, 401 *ushabti* were found: 365 to serve the deceased each day of the year, and 36 as overseers (one for every ten workers).

The *ushabti* figurines, which are sometimes elaborately modelled, help to recreate daily life in ancient Egypt by throwing light on its crafts, work in the fields and food preparation.

Ushabti, from the tomb of Tutankhamun, c.1330 BC. Egyptian Museum, Cairo. Along with other similar objects, these statuettes were placed in the tomb of the pharaoh, designed to carry out everyday tasks on behalf of the deceased in the afterlife.

The 'Mystery of the Pharaoh'

The sensational news of the discovery of the tomb of Tutankhamun and its treasures travelled around the world, trumpeted by newspapers and magazines, by photographic and cinematographic reports, and by the fledgling radio. By March 1923, more than 500 letters of congratulation had been received by Carter and Lord Carnarvon – although there were also letters critical of the desecration of the tomb – while journalists an d visitors were numerous and insistent.

As the objects were removed from the tomb a few at a time, they were photographed by reporters; the pictures were then published in the press, accompanied by extravagant commentary.

One event, which kept public interest alive in the excavation, was Lord Carnarvon's death, on 6th April, 1923, from a mosquito bite. The sudden and premature death of one of the first men to have set foot in the tomb of Tutankhamun after 33 centuries stimulated the imagination of the public, and the 'Curse of the Pharaohs' became not only the title of a highly influential newspaper article but also a subject of intense general speculation.

Lord Carnarvon, his daughter and Howard Carter by the tomb of Tut-ankhamun at the time of the discovery.

'A shiver is coursing through England...'

It was claimed that the words, 'Death Shall Come on Swift Wings To Him Who Disturbs the Peace of the King', were written on the tomb.

Six years after the death of Lord Carnarvon, Lord Westbury – who had acted as secretary to Carter during the excavations of the tomb – was found dead in his home in November, 1929, the precise cause remaining a mystery. The following year, Westbury's father committed suicide by throwing himself out of a seventh-floor window. If that was not enough, the hearse carrying the body of old Lord Westbury ran over and killed two boys in Battersea.

All of this was ascribed to the deadly power of Tutankhamun's curse. 'A shiver is coursing through England' was the sensational headline in the papers. The deaths of Arthur Cruttenden Mace, who had opened the burial chamber along with Carter, and the stepbrother of Lord Carnarvon, Aubrey Herbert, who committed suicide in a moment of 'spiritual enlightenment', caused further furore. And Lady Elisabeth Carnarvon also appeared to be a victim of Tutankhamun's wrath when, like her husband, she died as the result of an insect bite. The list of deaths attributed to the revenge of the pharaoh also included the names of Archibald Douglas Reid, who died just as he was preparing to X-ray a mummy, and the Egyptologist, Arthur Weigall, the twenty-first victim, who succumbed to an 'unknown fever'. Carter, who had more reason to fear the curse than any other, considered the whole story ridiculous, stating that the scientist 'should go about his work armed with respect and holy honesty, but without

Statuette of Tutankhamun, from the tomb of Tutankhamun, c.1330 BC. Egyptian

Museum, Cairo. The king is depicted on a boat, in the act of throwing a harpoon.

Imprint of a
seal with the
cartouche
of Tutankhamun,
c.1330 BC.
Newark
Museum,
Newark.

that fear which so easily takes
hold of the thrill-seeking
mob'. He died in 1939 at the
age of 66 – not a great age,

but why would the terrible
pharaoh have waited almost
twenty years before gaining
his revenge?

Chalice for the
immortality of
Tutankhamun,
from the
pharaoh's tomb,
c.1330 BC.
Egyptian
Museum, Cairo.

Model of a
boat, from
the tomb of
Tutankhamun,
c.1330 BC.
Egyptian
Museum,
Cairo. About
thirty models
were found
in the tomb,
representing
both ritual
boats and
boats used
on the Nile.

Gaston Maspero

Gaston Maspero (1846-1916), succeeded Mariette as Superintendant of the Egyptian Antiquities Service and as Director of the Cairo Museum, whose collection he catalogued in 50 volumes. He had contact with all the important archaeologists of the time (Loret, Petrie, Carter) and found benefactors and sponsors (i.g. Davis) when the funds of his institutions began to run out. In 1907 he encouraged the first archaeological expedition to Nubia, whose monuments had been almost forgotten. He was the first to publish the *Texts of the Pyramids*, and was the author of over 1,200 books and articles concerning Egypt.

Auguste Mariette

Auguste Mariette (1821-81), commissioned by the Louvre to acquire papyri in Egypt, remained there for the rest of his life. He was responsible for the discovery of the Serapeon at Saqqara, and the rediscovery of other important sites, fundamental to the study of the life of the ancient Egyptians. Mariette founded the Egyptian Museum at Bulak (transferred to Cairo in 1902) and was made Director of the Egyptian Antiquities Service. In his role as Inspector of Excavations, he established the first regulations for the defence of Egypt's heritage against the looting and indiscriminate exportation of treasures found during digging; subsequently, these artefacts – with the exception of a few 'honorary' gifts – became the property of the Cairo Museum.

Ancient and Modern Tomb Raiders

The temptation to steal the treasure of the pharaohs was irresistible even in ancient times. There are examples of sepulchres that are known to have been visited by thieves as soon as the funeral and internment had taken place.

As a result, the construction of tombs was carried out in great secret. An inscription on the walls of the burial chamber of the architect Ineni, from the time of the era of Thutmosis I, said: 'On my own did I direct the work of the secret tomb of the king. Nobody saw, nobody knew anything about it'.

The priests who protected the final resting place of the pharaohs sometimes succeeded in preventing a robbery, resealing the entrance to the tomb, as was the case with Tutankhamun.

In the modern era, the gold of pharaohs has made the fortune of many indigenous and foreign tomb raiders. On occasion, treasures found on the black market have even led archaeologists to a new site, by then irreparably gutted. Another form of theft was raiding by unscrupulous collectors, and the rapacity with which the colonial authorities exported the gold, treasures and papyri.

The first to seek to put an end to this 'authorised looting' were the inspector-archaeologists, Auguste Mariette and Gaston Maspero.

The treasure chamber of the tomb of Tutankhamun at the moment of its discovery. The objects had been placed in a random manner by ancient priests following an unsuccessful attempt to ransack the tomb.

Jewel box, from
the tomb of
Tutankhamun,
c.1330 BC.
Egyptian
Museum, Cairo.
The pharaoh
is depicted
on a chariot,
confronting and
defeating the
enemy armies of
the Syrians and
the Nubians.

THE REMAINS OF A CIVILIZATION
TUTANKHAMUN AND HIS TIME

View of the
Nile, the river
that profoundly
influenced the
development
of Egyptian
civilization.

Tutankhamun belonged to the Eighteenth Dynasty at the beginning of the New Kingdom, the most splendid era in the history of Egypt. Military conquests were matched by the arrival of vast riches from the occupied territories, which enriched the great temple complexes being developed in this period. New and magnificent buildings sprang up along the banks of the Nile, which continued to mark time with the repetition of its floods. Herodotus defined Egypt as the 'Gift of the Nile', but failed to mention that the prosperity of Egypt was also due to an efficient state organisation, the will of its governors, a love of art, respect for the gods and – above all – the labour of its workers.

Statuette of a
hippopotamus,
2064-1797 BC.
Egyptian
Museum,
Cairo. The
hippopotamus
was a familiar
sight in the
waters of the
Nile.

THE BLESSED LAND

Oasis of palm trees along the banks of the Nile. Landscapes such as this have hardly changed since ancient times.

All Egypt's history has been determined by its geography, which has allowed the country to remain isolated from its neighbours even while it has absorbed some aspects of their culture. The great expanses of desert to the east and west of the Nile served as one bulwark against invasion, and the cataracts of the river discouraged invasion from the south. From the north, the low and narrow Mediterranean coast and the marshy area of the Nile Delta offered protection. Life flourished, therefore, both in the delta and along the Nile valley. Together these constituted a sort of fertile oasis more than 1,200 kilometres in length, which the Egyptians called 'Black Land' (kemi), after the colour of the soil, darkened by lime deposits. Beyond this zone are the 'Red Lands' of the Libyan and Arabian deserts. The Libyan Desert to the west is prevalently flat and open, with a series of oases arranged more or less in parallel with the course of the Nile. The Arabian Desert is a plateau, crossed by ancient, deep, dried-up riverbeds (wadi), where life of any kind is limited. The Egyptians called the land between the delta and Memphis Lower Egypt, while the valley itself, from Memphis to the first cataract Aswan, was known as Upper Egypt. Due to the great river, the cultivation of the land had a pre-eminent role in Egypt and the country was like a vast agricultural plant, with a productivity that was extremely high for the time. None of this would have been possible without the regular inundations of the river, which appeared like the gift of beneficent gods.

Brief Notes on the Chronology of Ancient Egypt

ANCIENT KINGDOM (2686-2160 BC): development of the pre-eminence of the pharaohs and the construction of the first great pyramids.

I INTERMEDIATE PERIOD (2160-2055 BC): a period of crisis, which witnessed the fragmentation of the country into many local principalities.

MIDDLE KINGDOM (2055-1650 BC): the reunification of Upper and Lower Egypt, and the beginning of a period characterised by long, peaceful reigns.

II INTERMEDIATE PERIOD (1650-1550 BC): a new period of crisis, which saw a weakening of central power and the expansion of a foreign population known as the Hyksos.

NEW KINGDOM (1550-1069 BC): the period of greatest splendour, with Egyptian supremacy at home and abroad accompanied by the construction of the largest temple buildings in the whole of Egypt.

III INTERMEDIATE PERIOD (1069-664 BC): the collapse of the dynasty of the Ramses, and the consequent new division of Egypt.

LATE ERA (664-332 BC): a period characterised by a series of foreign occupations, with the conquest of Alexander the Great signalling the definitive loss of Egyptian autonomy.

Polychromatic reliefs with scenes showing the gathering of papyrus, grazing and hunting, c. 2450 BC. Saqqara, Mastaba of Nefer and Ka-hay.

Opposite: Stele of King Ahmose, 1550-1525 BC. Egyptian Museum, Cairo. The pharaoh was once again sovereign of both Upper and Lower Egypt, after a period of instability due to the domination of the Hyksos.

THE NEW KINGDOM

The millenary history of
Egypt can be subdivided
into three great epochs:
the Ancient Kingdom, the
Middle Kingdom and the New
Kingdom, interrupted by two
Intermediate Periods. The era of
Tutankhamun and his dynasty
(the Eighteenth) falls within the
New Kingdom, which was a
period of enormous splendour
for the whole of Egypt. The
Eighteenth Dynasty marked a
change after two centuries of
domination by the Hyksos, who
came from the west to settle in
the Nile Delta. The harsh rule of
these people weakened as the
new dynasty began to oppose
them. The Sixteenth and the
Seventeenth Dynasties were
essentially of the same stock
and time as the Fourteenth
and Fifteenth Dynasties. Their
princes continued to reign over
Thebes, refusing to recognise
the power of the Hyksos and,
whenever possible, opposing

Pharaoh Amenhotep II on a chariot, 1427-1400 BC. Museum of Ancient Egyptian Art, Luxor. The war chariot was introduced to Egypt by the Hyksos invaders.

The Hyksos

An ancient Semitic people, with origins in Asia, who the Egyptians called 'Hyksos' (from 'hekakhesut', meaning 'subjects of the sovereign of another people'). They began to invade the country, via the Sinai Peninsula, about 1700 BC, and founded their own dynasties (the Fourteenth and Fifteenth) in opposition to those of the Egyptians. In 1674 BC, under the Thirteenth Egyptian Dynasty, they besieged Memphis, but elected Avari, in the delta, as their capital.

Although it was defined as an invasion, the advance of the Hyksos came about without great conflict: their numbers increased until they dominated Lower Egypt. They introduced horses and war chariots, which the Egyptians were subsequently to use against them.

them. But it was the Theban prince, Kahmose, a devotee of Amon, who was most responsible for reawakening Egyptian consciousness when he declared war on the Hyksos in 1550 BC. Kahmose fell prematurely in battle but his role was taken over by his brother, Ahmose, who founded the dynasty which completed the defeat of the Hyksos and reunited Upper and Lower Egypt in a single sovereign state. This initiated the New

Kingdom (1550-1069 BC), which would see the succession of the Eighteenth, Nineteenth and Twentieth Dynasties. The experience of foreign domination had left the population and its rulers with a great desire for security, which would push it over the centuries to endeavour to conquer the countries on its borders. This expansionism brought contact with other peoples and, as a consequence, trade.

Fresco showing peoples conquered by Egypt bearing tributes to the pharaoh, c. 1550-1069 BC. Tomb of the Nobles, Thebes.

For decades, splendid treasures seized in battle, the tributes of vassal states, and the valuable goods of merchants entered Egypt in vast quantities. Such riches began to have a significant impact. The capital, Thebes, was expanded and invested with unprecedented architectural magnificence. The temples dedicated to the gods overflowed with offers and treasure. The size of the population grew with the economy.

Relief showing prisoners with their hands tied behind their backs, c.1550-1069 BC. Luxor. Representations such as these served to propagandise Egyptian conquests in neighbouring countries.

The ceremonial axe of King Ahmose, 1550-1525 BC. Egyptian Museum, Cairo. This sovereign was the founder of the Eighteenth Dynasty, which inaugurated the New Kingdom.

THE POLITICAL SYSTEM OF THE STATE

The Egyptian state had always had a centralised, hierarchical structure. Power was firmly in the hands of the king or pharaoh. He outlined government policy and promoted state initiatives, but delegated a large amount of his executive power to the vizier, the head of the extremely efficient administration. The vizier was assisted by the heads of the principal sectors, who made up the upper class of functionaries. These acted as the delegates of the king, interpreting his will and spreading it throughout the country via local functionaries, who administered justice, finance, agriculture, public works and so on. The functionaries of every rank and level responded faithfully and promptly to their superiors, and exercised power over their inferiors judiciously.

The social regime of the Egyptian state was fluid, allowing for a continuous movement of managers from one category to another, and with the dominant class accepting the influx of the able, even if their origins were humble. This replacement took place slowly, without revolution or political upheaval, to enable the new managers to acquire the skills and abilities of their predecessors.

Relief portrait of the vizier Ramose, c.1360-1350 BC. Tomb of Ramose, Thebes. The vizier had the highest position in the government of the kingdom after the pharaoh.

The Pharaoh: Order, Prosperity and Harmony

The symbol and sustenance of the state was the pharaoh, incarnation of the goddess Maat, guaranteeing continuity and happiness in the country. He was the intermediary between the human and divine worlds, guarantor of the permanence of the Order and Harmony of the Cosmos, and without whose intervention there would be Chaos. With the magical forces that emanated from him, the pharaoh ensured the fertility of the land, the prosperity of his subjects, and the strength of his armies. His authority was unlimited and unchallenged. As the spiritual son of Maat, he proclaimed decrees which were evidently just and well-balanced – being divinely inspired – but it was the vizier who had the responsibility for making sure these laws were respected: human error could not be allowed to alter divine justice. Similarly, religious authority, innate in the pharaoh, was delegated to the class of priests who were given the task of substituting for him in the celebration of rites. Egypt had a large number of gods and the sacred ceremonies called for a great number of temple employees. Large tracts of land bestowed by the pharaoh were often involved and the priests had a variety of jobs as administrators, production heads, maintenance supervisors and so on. They were formed into rigorous hierarchies, culminating in the title 'Servant of the God' or 'High Priest of the Temple'.

Statue of Thutmosis III, pharaoh of the Eighteenth Dynasty, from Karnak, c.1450 BC. Museum of Ancient Egyptian Art, Luxor.

Bust of
Amenemhet III
in priestly garb,
from Faiyum,
c.1800 BC.
Egyptian
Museum, Cairo.
The pharaoh
was the highest
political and
religious power
in the state,
but many tasks
were entrusted
to the vizier and
priesthood.

Sphinx of
Amenemhet III,
c.1800 BC.
Egyptian
Museum, Cairo.
The comparison
of the power of
the sovereign
to the strength
and force of a
lion was not
unusual in
ancient Egypt.

Colossal head of Akhenaten with the double crown, in profile, c.1350 BC. Museum of Ancient Egyptian Art, Luxor.

The 'Sed' Jubilee Festivities

The Sed Festivities were usually celebrated after 30 years of the pharaoh's reign, and commemorated the anniversary of his crowning with a view to renewing the power of the sovereign and his government.
The pharaoh, with the double-crown of the Upper and Lower Kingdoms on his head, followed a precise ritual four times in a row (one for each of the cardinal points of the compass), thereby symbolically renewing his possession of Egypt.

The Court

The pharaoh lived with his family at the 'Great House', which was both an official residence and a place in which to offer hospitality to important guests. There were three grades of queen – the 'queen mother', the 'king's wives' and the 'great wife of the king', mother of the heir to the throne – plus concubines with their numerous children. Also present were the pharaoh's intimate friends, who were known as the 'relatives of the king', the children of allied sovereigns, and several functionaries who had either made themselves indispensable or had distinguished themselves in military campaigns.

The court included both the employees of the royal family (butlers, chambermaids, hairdressers and perfume artists, manicurists, doctors and so on) and craftsmen in their service (sculptors, cabinetmakers, goldsmiths, tailors and others). There were also noblewomen, the wives of important dignitaries, who formed a sisterhood under the protection of Hathor, the cow-goddess wet nurse of the kings.

The pharaoh was a remote and untouchable figure, even for the courtesans who squabbled over the smallest sign of consideration and struggled to obtain any kind of honorary title, even if it was meaningless. The god-king appeared in public only during the great ceremonies, which were codified by a rigid protocol.

Stele of the family of Akhenaten with the solar disc, and a detail of the daughters of the pharaoh, 1340 BC. Egyptian Museum, Cairo.

The Priests: Servants of the God

Among the 'VIPs' of the bureaucratic apparatus were the members of the High Priesthood, who were delegated by the pharaoh – the premier priest – to celebrate the rites. There existed a rigid hierarchy and a precise subdivision of responsibilities. In every sanctuary there was a head priest, called 'prophet', who officiated at the rites as the representative of the pharaoh. The minor clergy was made up of 'uebu', the 'pure', employed in the maintenance of sacred artefacts and of the temple. There were also female personnel, the 'uebuit', who were directed by the queen. The person of the priest did not alter substantially from

Statue of the priest Kaaper, known as 'Sheikh el Beledd', from Saqqara, c. 2450 BC. Egyptian Museum, Cairo.

The statue shows the appearance of a priest, which remained unchanged through centuries.

the Ancient to the Middle to the New Kingdoms: he was shaven-headed, depilated and circumcised; dressed in pure linen; obliged to avoid all sexual contact while in the service of the temple (three months a year); and well-versed in theology. He might be a great administrator; a first, second, third or fourth prophet of the god; or perhaps a purifier or a scribe; or an astronomer who fixed the moment for ceremonies, and was specialised in recognising the most propitious or inauspicious days; a cantor, harpist, flautist or trumpet player. By the era of the New Kingdom, the priests of Amon at Thebes exercised a strong political influence. In effect, they set up their own independent kingdom in Upper Egypt. Women were given a temporary role as 'sacred singers' and, from the end of the New Kingdom, that of 'divine spouse of Amon', or 'worshipper of the god' – which was also the destiny of one of the king's daughters, who had to remain a virgin. She would have to adopt a young princess as her heir. The 'divine spouse' was also surrounded by a harem of virgins, all adoptive mothers of girls destined to take their place. Apart from the festivities and honours, they were also entitled to 1000 hectares of land, situated in various parts of Upper Egypt and the Nile Delta.

The Upper Echelons of the Hierarchy

The highest-ranking functionaries were the 'mer', 'those who have the mouthpiece', who as departmental ministers controlled the king or vizier's inspectors. In every department there were also numerous inferior ranks, such as secretaries, scribes and archivists. Governors, nominated directly by the pharaoh from the local population and appointed or dismissed at his pleasure, were in charge of the provinces ('nòmoi') or administrative areas. They were assisted by a 'referendary' who, at the edges of the kingdom, exercised the same function as the vizier at the centre.

In Upper Egypt there were always 22 provinces, while in Lower Egypt their number varied from 13 to 17. Governors with special police powers administered the western oases, which were subject to Libyan raids. These men were chosen from the military ranks, and only rarely succeeded in gaining honour because Egypt, protected by the sea and the desert, rarely had to fight in order to defend itself.

Walls illustrating a procession of functionaries, c.1450 BC. Tomb of the vizier Rekhmire, Sheikh Abd-el Qurna.

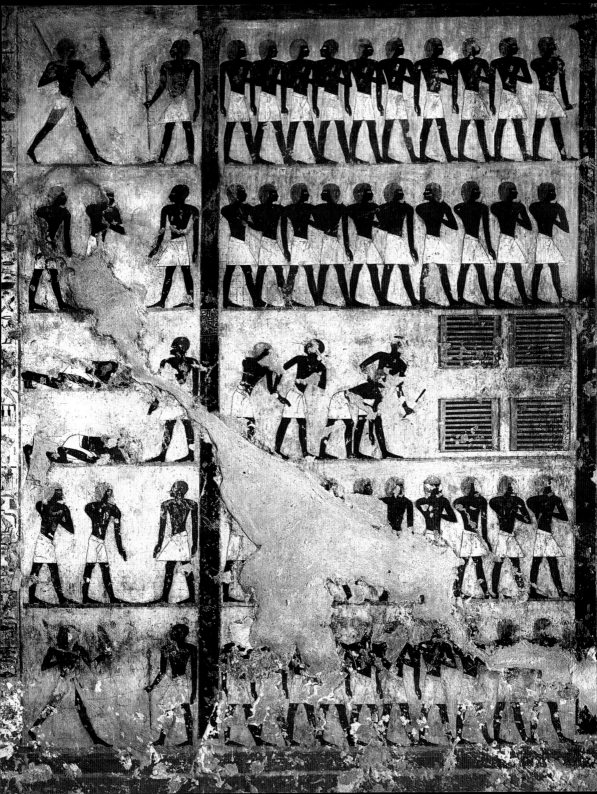

The Scribes: Omnipresent and Scrupulous

Alongside the high functionaries close to the pharaoh were the lower-ranking, executive bureaucrats: the scribes.

The scribes were numerous and characteristic of Egypt because no other ancient civilization had such a literate administration. All scribes had learnt the complicated Egyptian writing systems – the sacred system of hieroglyphics and the simpler hieratic system – but although the humbler among them would spend their lives writing down the dictated orders of higher-ranking functionaries, others were trusted with much greater responsibility and intervened in all areas of public life.

They were present in central and regional administrative offices; in the fields taking measurements, counting livestock or assessing crops; at the frontier to control trading and foreign visitors; and everywhere in order to collect taxes. The very survival of the population depended on the precision and competence of their work. Not only was it their duty to censor and calculate acquired wealth, they also had to mitigate the impact of bad years, when excessive or inadequate inundations might lead to famine, by setting up and maintaining emergency supplies.

Statue of a
seated scribe,
c. 2470 BC.
Egyptian
Museum,
Cairo.

Renowned Egyptian Pharaohs

The New Kingdom is notable for the strong personality of its sovereigns, who left their mark on the country's history. They were gifted with political foresight and motivated by a desire for conquest.

Thutmosis III (Eighteenth Dynasty), for example, conducted about twenty military campaigns, extending the borders of the kingdom to include Nubia, Libya, Syria and Mesopotamia. Seti I (Nineteenth Dynasty) victoriously confronted Hittites, Syrians and Libyans, while one of his successors, Ramses III, in addition to the customary conflicts with the Libyans, had to test himself against the so-called 'Peoples of the Sea', who represented a real threat to the security of Egypt.

The presence of able and resolute sovereigns was one of the principal factors, which ensured that the New Kingdom was an era of such legendary splendour. The great wealth of the period could, however, lead to the reawakening of special interests. The wealth of the priests of Amon, protected by the first sovereigns of the Eighteenth Dynasty, eventually led to discontent among the aristocracy, who favoured the religious revolution of Amenhotep IV. This eventually affirmed the cult of the god Aten.

Statue of Thutmosis III, kneeling, c.1450 BC. Egyptian Museum, Cairo.

This sovereign was the conqueror of numerous neighbouring peoples.

The 'Peoples of the Sea'

In about 1200 BC, the Hittite
Empire was overrun by the
'Peoples of the Sea', which
then turned their attention,
in sequential waves, towards
the Nile Delta. They were
a confederation of tribes,
whose names are indicative
of their Mediterranean
origin: Sherden (Sardinians),
Shekelesh (Sicans-Sikels),
Lukka (Lycians), Danuna
(Danaoi), Tursha (Tyrrhenians,
Etruscans), Peleset
(Philistines or Palestinians).
   They were probably led
by the Akhaluasha (the
Achaei). They were defeated
definitively by Ramses
III (1184-1153 BC) of the
Twentieth Dynasty.

Ramses III
(the pharaoh
who defeated
the 'Peoples
of the Sea')
in front of

the Gods of
Memphis,
c. 1150 BC.
British
Museum,
London.

Colossal
statue of
Amenhotep IV
(or Akhenaten)
from Karnak,
c. 1350 BC.
Egyptian
Museum, Cairo.

This pharaoh
was the driving
force behind
the religious
revolution
that led to the
monotheistic
cult of Aten.

Shadow and Light
in the Eighteenth Dynasty

Below and opposite: *Colossi of Memnone*, c.1360 BC. Thebes. These gigantic sculptures are all that remain of the funerary temple of Amenhotep III.

The sovereigns of this dynasty knew how to forge an able managerial class and succeeded in both establishing an empire and ruling it solidly. The foreign policy of the era was dominated by the continuation of the war in the east against the Hurrites and the kingdom of Mitannians, and by substantiating possession of northern Nubia while pursuing conquest in the south. Within the country there was a dynastic crisis provoked by Queen Hatshepsut, but confined to the upper hierarchies of the state.

In 1479 BC, Thutmosis III ascended to the throne as co-regent, a situation that persisted for 22 years. Between the 22nd and 44th years of his reign he conducted 17 military campaigns, which extended Egyptian power as far as Mesopotamia. The whole of the Levante was under its hegemony and organised into provinces.

After the death of Thutmosis III, Egyptian policies in the Levante became much less expansive. The first sovereign of this phase was Thutmosis IV.

Amenhotep III kept the peace within his borders for more than 30 years (1390-1352 BC). Of his vast funerary temple in the plain of western Thebes, only two statues of the king remain, the Colossi of Memnone. The religious crisis prompted by Amenhotep IV shook the entire administrative structure and distracted attention from the western empire.

Chronology of the Eighteenth Dynasty

1550-1525	AHMOSE
1525-1504	AMENHOTEP I
1504-1492	THUTMOSIS I
1492-1479	THUTMOSIS II
1479-1425	THUTMOSIS III
1473-1458	HATSHEPSUT
1427-1400	AMENHOTEP II
1400-1390	THUTMOSIS IV
1390-1352	AMENHOTEP III
1352-1336	AMENHOTEP IV (AKHENATEN)
1338-1336	SMENKHARA
1336-1327	TUTANKHAMUN
1327-1323	AY
1323-1295	HOREMHEB

Pharaoh
Thutmosis IV
received as a
god, c. 1390 BC.
Tomb of
Thutmosis IV,
Valley of the
Kings.

Temple of
Hatshepsut at
Deir el-Bahari,
c.1460 BC.

The Temple of Queen Hatshepsut

Hatshepsut had her own
funerary temple built at Deir
el-Bahari, next to that of
Nebhepetra Mentuhotpe,
pharaoh of the Middle
Kingdom. It is more a series
of colonnades – one on top
of another, with access
gained via ramps – than a true
temple. On the walls of the
lowest colonnade, some badly
damaged blocks illustrate
the transportation by ship
of two obelisks from Aswan
to Karnak. To the right there
remains just one engraved
image of Hatshepsut as a
sphinx. On the left there is the
representation of an expedition
to the land of Punt, the region
in the Horn of Africa where the
Egyptians procured incense,
ivory, wood and gold. In its
corner there is a small temple
dedicated to Hathor, with
coloured reliefs depicting the
queen being breastfed by the
goddess in the form of a cow.
Another colonnade presents
the conception, birth and
childhood of Hatshepsut. At
its end lies the small chapel
dedicated to Anubis, decorated
with magnificent paintings.
When the new sovereign,
Thutmosis III, ascended to
the throne, he ordered the
demolition of the monument
to his stepmother, that
'scandalous usurper' of divine
power.

Hatshepsut: the Woman who Declared Herself King

The daughter of
Thutmosis I and of Queen
Ahmes, Hatshepsut
(1473-1458 BC) was destined
from an early age to marry
her stepbrother Thutmosis II,
born of a concubine, with the
sole purpose of legitimising
his ascension to the throne.

Widowed in 1474 BC,
Hatshepsut was nominated
regent for her stepson and
son-in-law Thutmosis III.
In a short time, however,
the strong-willed princess
managed to concentrate all
power in her hands, and
to effectively assume the
role of sovereign of Egypt,
declaring herself pharaoh in
1473 BC. From that moment
she would be portrayed in
statues and monuments with
exclusively male features,
including the ritual beard.
During the years of her reign,
Hatshepsut progressively
abandoned her father's
the expansionist policies,
increasingly dedicating her
time to internal affairs. With
the help and advice of her
favourite, the architect,
Senmut, she commissioned
the building of the grandiose
temple at Deir el-Bahari. On
the death of Hatshepsut,
Thutmosis III ruthlessly
eliminated her from memory,
giving orders to destroy all
her statues and to cancel her
name from the Royal Lists.

Following
pages: Relief
of Queen
Hatshepsut
(left) depicted
as pharaoh,
celebrating the
raising of a pair
of obelisks in
honour of the
god Amon, from
the Pink Chapel
of Hatshepsut
at Karnak,
c.1460 BC.
Museum
of Ancient
Egyptian Art,
Luxor.

Head of Queen
Hatshepsut
c.1460 BC, from
Deir el-Bahari.
Egyptian
Museum, Cairo.

The Fist of Thutmosis III

Thutmosis III was the greatest military leader and politician of ancient Egypt. Of his seventeen military campaigns, ten were simply shows of strength, but seven were true wars: the victory over Megiddo, where the king's innovative tactical plan helped to defeat this powerful stronghold in the southern Levante; the conquest of Kadesh on the Oronte, another enemy bastion; the subjugation of the Phoenician cities, intended to ensure support from the sea for his armies marching north, again tactically radical; the capture of Karkemish on the Euphrates; the advance along the Euphrates as far as the Taurus Mountains; the repression of the revolt by the Hurrites and their allies with the victory at Aleppo; the putting down of the revolt of Kadesh (perhaps the one on the Oronte, or maybe a homonymous city in Galilee) and of Tunip (another city in Galilee).

Thutmosis III,
in the act of
worshipping
Amon-Ra,
c.1450 BC.
Chapel of
Hathor,
Deir el-Bahari.

Amenhotep IV
the Heretic

Halfway through the
Eighteenth Dynasty, Prince
Thutmosis, eldest son of King
Amenhotep III and Queen Tiy,
died unexpectedly, which
drew attention to his younger
brother. Little is known about
this prince. He lived for many
years at Memphis, with his
mother's brother, Ay, as a
friend and advisor. For four
years he was co-regent with
his father, Amenhotep III,
who the first sovereign to
promote the cult of Aten,
the solar god of Heliopolis
– depicted at Karnak as a
falcon with a disc in the form
of the sun on its head.

When he became king,
Amenhotep IV changed his
name to Akenaten. He was
already married to Princess
Nefertiti, whom some
considered to be a foreigner
but others believed to be
the daughter of Ay and his
wife Tey. The young king
soon displayed his aversion
to Egyptian traditions. In

Relief of
Akhenaten and
Nefertiti making
offerings to the
god Aten, from
Tel el-Amarna,
c.1340 BC
Egyptian
Museum, Cairo.

the fourth or fifth year of
his reign he repudiated
Amon, ordering all effigies
of the god be destroyed and
proclaimed Aten as the only
supreme god. He tolerated the
presence of other divinities
only if they were considered
manifestations of Aten.

In the sixth year of his reign,
he transferred the capital
from Thebes to Tel el-Amarna,
and gave it the new name of
Akhetaten ('City of the Horizon
of Aten'). Here Aten is depicted
in the form of the sun, with
rays terminating in hands, on
which appear the hieroglyphic
symbols representing life and
power. This image is often
described as 'a solar disc', but
the inscriptions make it quite
clear that the king considered
Aten to be the creative force
behind the universe, of which
the sun was a symbol. The god
did not have his own image.

But the time was not ready
for the abolition of theocratic
power, especially as the priests

Relief featuring
Ay and Tey
receiving
the 'golden
recompense'
from Akhenaten,
Tel el-Amarna,
c.1340 BC.
Egyptian
Museum, Cairo.
A large part of the
evidence relating
to Akhenaten
comes from
Tel el-Amarna, the
capital founded
by the heretical
pharaoh, and
named Akhetaten
('City of the
Horizon of Aten').

Picture of ducks in a papyrus marsh, from Tel el-Amarna, c.1340 BC. Egyptian Museum, Cairo.

Tel el-Amarna was short-lived, being abandoned after the death of the sovereign.

of Amon still wielded enough influence to challenge even the pharaoh. When it became clear that Akhetaten's lack of interest in foreign affairs had gravely compromised the situation in the outlying provinces, the priests of Amon decided to take action, imposing a change of direction on the sovereign. The king died in the seventeenth year of his reign.

The City of
the Horizon of Aten

Statuette of
Akhenaten
in the act of
making an
offering, from
Tel el-Amarna,
c.1340 BC.
Egyptian
Museum,
Cairo.

Akhetaten, corresponding to today's el-Amarna, was subdivided into different areas. To the west were the apartments of the functionaries, with halls and great courtyards decorated with enormous statues of the king and queen. A bridge formed a balcony, where the royal family made state appearances, and this was connected to the private apartments, which rose on the other side. To the south of them was a small temple dedicated to Aten, probably for the king's use. To the north, a series of warehouses separated the palace from the main temple, which dominated the city. In an immense open-air courtyard there were several stone tables, which served as altars, where offerings of food and drink could be left for Aten. On the western side of this courtyard, a small sanctuary was built, probably used only by Akhenaten and

his High Priest. In a later era a smaller structure was added, near the entrance on the western side of the courtyard. This was called Gem-Aten, meaning 'Aten is found again'. There was also a colonnaded hall known as the 'House of Joy'. To the east of the palace and temple arose the principal administrative offices, including the office for foreign affairs, where hundreds of clay tablets were found in 1891-92. North of the temple, in the northern 'suburbs', were private homes. Many of them were extremely luxurious, with gardens, swimming pools surrounded by trees, and private baths. The houses of the poor were crowded in amongst them, often exploiting existing walls to support their new ones.

North of the city, beyond a canal, which carried the city's wastewater to the Nile, a palace that would appear to have belonged to

Tablet with cuneiform inscription, from Tel el-Amarna, c.1370-1350 BC. British Museum, London.

Documents like this allow us to reconstruct the brief history of the city founded by Akhenaten.

Queen Nefertiti was built. At some distance to the south was the Meru-Aten, a magnificently spacious, airy construction surrounded by

trees, with rooms painted in bright colours, used by the women of the royal family as a place for relaxation, away from the city centre.

Tutankhamun, the Boy Pharaoh

Tutankhamun ('Perfects the Life of Amon' or 'Living Image of Amon') appears in the Egyptian universe like a comet; what little information exists about his life only refers to the six years of his reign. He was probably the son of the heretic pharaoh, Akhenaten, and died at the age of 18 without having had time to distinguish himself in any great enterprise. Nevertheless, he was the instigator, along with his counsellors, of a return to traditional ways, after the heretical radicalism of his predecessor.

On the death of Akhenaten, the key player became the priest Ay, tutor of the youthful pharaoh, who had reconverted to the faith of Amon. Tutankhamun was forced to move the capital back

Fragment of the Pillar of Akhenaten, from Karnak, c.1340 BC. Egyptian Museum, Cairo. The heretical pharaoh was the predecessor, and probably the father, of Tutankhamun.

to Thebes – even though he resided in Memphis – and to reinstate the ancient cult. The temples of Aten were razed to the ground and Tutankhamun lavished rich treasures on the priests to compensate them for the damage done to them by his father. He married Princess Ankhesenpaaton, daughter of Akhenaten and Nefertiti. After his death, the priest-tutor Ay married his widow and became pharaoh for a brief time, on a throne, which was becoming less steady.

It is perhaps Ay's mania for grandeur, which ensured for Tutankhamun the fame that is a kind of eternal life. Ay took possession of the imposing funerary monument that had been got ready for Tutankhamun in the Valley of the Kings, exchanging it for his own, rather more humble, tomb. It was precisely thanks to the modest size of this that, after an initial attempt at looting, Tutankhamun ended up buried and forgotten for centuries.

In Egyptian chronicles, the vicissitudes of Akhenaten and Tutankhamun were recorded rather briefly, as if it was felt they were best forgotten. Both the artistic revolution – characterised by the realistic depiction of people and the exaltation of their natural features – and the religious revolution – with the creation of the god, Aten – came to an end with the death of Akhenaten, the 'heretical' pharaoh.

Relief of
Tutankhamun,
detail,
c.1330 BC.
Temple of
Amon-Ra,
Luxor.

Ramses II: a Giant in the History of Egypt

The end of the second millennium BC begins the era of the Warrior Pharaohs, the Nineteenth Dynasty of the Ramessidi, able to thwart the territorial ambitions of the Hittites and the 'Peoples of the Sea'.

On the throne for 66 years, from 1279 to 1213 BC, Ramses II is considered one of the greatest pharaohs in history. His name remains linked to a whole series of events and monuments that contributed to the splendour of the Egypt of the New Kingdom.

Extraordinary building activity took place during his years of government: he was probably responsible for the construction of the magnificent city of Pi-Ramesse, in the western part of the Nile Delta, and the two rocky temples at Abu Simbel and the majestic Theban edifices, such as the Ramesseum, still survive.

Caught up in an epic struggle with the Hittites, which culminated in the historic battle of Kadesh, on the Oronte, with neither side a clear victor; Ramses signed the first 'non-aggression pact'

Opposite:
Statue of
Ramses II,
c.1270 BC.
Egyptian
Museum, Turin.

Facade of
the Temple
of Ramses II,
c.1250 BC.
Abu Simbel.

in history with the sovereign of the Hittites, Hattusili III. To consolidate this agreement, the pharaoh married two Hittite princesses, who joined the sovereign's already crowded and cosmopolitan harem. His favourite wives were Nefertari and Isisnofret, and he chose his heir, Merenptah, from among the children of the latter. Many historians identify Ramses II as the pharaoh of the Exodus.

THE GREAT QUEENS

Portrait of
Nefertiti, from
Tel el-Amarna,
c.1340 BC.
Egyptian
Museum, Cairo.
Nefertiti was
the wife of
the celebrated
heretical
pharaoh,
Akhenaten.

In a country with a patriarchal structure, women can appear of little importance, despite the sporadic presence of female pharaohs.

The queens generally lived in the shadow of the sovereign, who owned a crowded harem and numerous concubines. It was not uncommon for marriages to be contracted with close blood relatives (brother and sister, father and daughter), making the bonds of family even tighter.

Nevertheless, some queens have left their mark, either as protagonists, or through exercising significant influence over their regal consort; others again, endowed with particular beauty, have become the stuff of legend: this is the case with Nefertiti, of whom several portraits have come down to us. It is also true for the last celebrated Queen of Egypt, Cleopatra, first linked with Julius Caesar and then with Mark Anthony, for whose sake she took her own life in 30 BC.

There were a number of women with strong personalities among the ancestors of Tutankhamun, who helped guide the Eighteenth Dynasty through a period of great transformation.

The first was Tetisheri, progenitor of the family line, followed by Ahhotep, mother of the pharaoh Ahmose, conqueror of the Hyksos, who held the reigns of government whilst her son was at war. On the death of Ahmose, it was his wife, Nefertari, who guided the kingdom during the years of Egypt's massive expansion, while her son, Amenhotep I, was too young to govern. The highly celebrated Queen Hatshepsut was admired for her resolve.

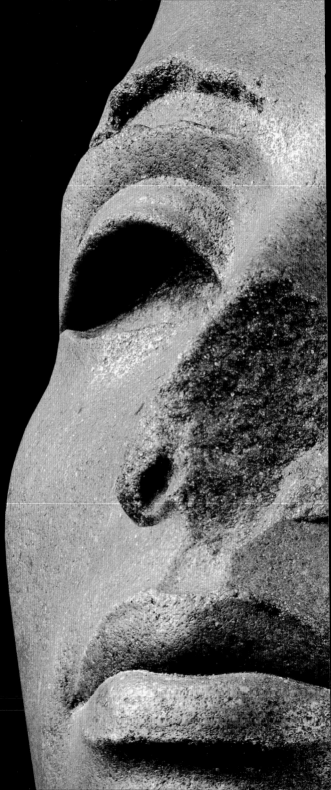

The Pilfering of Nefertiti

In 1912, Ludwig Borchard, who directed the works of the Deutsche Orient Gesellschaft at el-Amarna, had the good fortune to come across the workshop of a sculptor called Thutmosi, where he discovered works of art and models of exceptional interest. Among these was the head of Queen Nefertiti in polychrome limestone. With clever and manoeuvring, all the pieces ended up in the Museum of Berlin. This virtual theft by a famous scientific institute led to a diplomatic row, which has never been resolved.

Copy of the bust of Queen Nefertiti, the original of which is in Berlin. Egyptian Museum, Florence.

Nefertiti the Beautiful

Nefertiti, the lovely young wife of Amenhotep IV, was blessed with a name that meant 'Beauty has arrived'. For many years she was considered a foreigner; it is more likely, however, that she was an Egyptian noblewoman, who became legendary on account of her breathtaking beauty when she supported her husband in the difficult religious reforms he undertook. A fervent follower of the cult of Aten, the queen always appears at her husband's side when he is depicted in his priestly role.

Nefertiti remained faithful to Aten even after the priests of Amon had forced her husband to repudiate the god. Removing herself to the northern part of Akhetaten, in a palace called the Castle of Aten, the queen lived in a kind of voluntary exile until the end of her days. For this reason, some believe that Nefertiti was rejected by Akhenaten, who may have preferred the youth, Smenkhara.

Statue of Akhenaten and Nefertiti, c.1340 BC. Musée du Louvre, Paris.

Statue of
a woman,
perhaps
Nefertiti,
c.1340 BC.
Musée du
Louvre, Paris.

Nefertari's Glamour

Halls with painted walls from the interior of the tomb of Nefertari, Twelfth century BC, Thebes. Nefertari was the wife of the pharaoh Ramses II, and held a position of power in the running of the country.

Nefertari was one of the numerous wives of pharaoh Ramses II. Her name is the superlative of the adjective 'nefer', which in Egyptian means 'beautiful'; thus it can be translated as 'Very Beautiful' or 'Most Beautiful'.

Nefertari took on this name when she got married, and it is likely that she did so for dynastic motives. 'The Beauty of Glamour', as some of her epitaphs call her, was loved and respected by Ramses II to such an extent that the pharaoh dedicated a temple at Abu Simbel to her; and in several *bas reliefs* and statuary groups, she is represented as the same size as the pharaoh, which was exceptional in Egyptian art. The titles on her tomb suggest that she enjoyed a highly respected position in the hierarchy. She was called 'irit pat', which means 'hereditary princess', implying that she had a claim to regency. According to a hypothesis of Schiaparelli, Nefertari might have been the daughter of the pharaoh Ay, the penultimate pharaoh of the Eighteenth Dynasty, because a lotus flower in deep blue enamel with the cartouche of Ay was found in the burial hall of the queen.

The Art of the New Kingdom

Colossal
head of
Amenhotep III,
from Qurna,
c.1360 BC.
Museum
of Ancient
Egyptian Art,
Luxor. With
the reign of
Amenhotep III,
predecessor
of Akhenaten,
Egypt reached
the apex of its
political power
and artistic
refinement.

Under Amenhotep III, who reigned for 38 years, the country reached the apex not only of its political power, but also of the refinement of its art. In sculpture, the formality of previous periods was replaced by an aesthetic search aimed at providing delight, and characterised by the cult of physical beauty. Profiles became more sinuous; the details of faces and clothes were reproduced with great care. *Bas-reliefs* were embellished by a palette of colours and a variety of themes. Alongside work scenes there appeared others depicting historical moments, such as those representing the tributary processions of foreigners.

The art of the Amarna Period (1352-36 BC) has instantly recognisable characteristics. The king and his wife Nefertiti are portrayed worshipping the solar disc, the royal family depicted with long bodies and slender limbs, elongated heads and oval faces, and large, almond-shaped eyes. This type of representation was aimed at conferring upon the sovereign and his family expressions of deep spirituality.

Monumental sculpture, as well as the minor arts, displayed a luminous sensitivity, with extreme delicacy of surfaces. These characteristics are also to be found in the art of Tutankhamun's brief reign.

With the Nineteenth Dynasty, the Theban clan reached the end of its line, and, as seen above, a series of general-kings, the Ramessidians, took power. Thebes was abandoned once more in favour of the ancient city of Memphis. Building work flourished, and the great temples at Luxor and Karnak were constructed.

In *bas-reliefs*, historical narration became popular. Military triumphs were recorded, often with great

Portrait of a princess, from Tel el-Amarna, c.1340 BC. Egyptian Museum, Cairo. The portraits of pharaoh Akhenaten, his wife Nefertiti and their family clearly illustrate the new styles in the art of the Amarna period.

attention to detail and descriptive realism. Particularly celebrated are the annals of Ramses II at Karnak, which depict the Battle of Kadesh. In sculpture, compositional forms multiplied, with such a vogue for complex, intellectual forms that there is talk of 'Ramessidian Baroque'. Contrast was admired, with the ample, plain textures of the faces juxtaposed against the restless *chiaroscuro* of the elaborate wigs and heavily folded clothes. The work of artisans also flourished, particularly that of goldsmithing and enamelled ceramics.

Statue of Ramses II, c.1260 BC. Temple of Amon-Ra, Karnak. Under the kings of this clan, the mighty temple complexes of Karnak and Luxor reached their greatest splendour.

Opposite: Obelisk and colossal statue, Eighth century BC. Temple of Amon-Ra, Luxor, Both the temple complexes at Thebes were dedicated to the cult of Amon-Ra.

Thebes: the Great Capital

The capital of Imperial Egypt was Thebes, where the sovereign traditionally resided, surrounded by the hierarchical administrative apparatus. Apart from the functionaries, priests and military classes – these, by this stage, reinforced by generations of military campaigns – the city also acted as a magnet for the emerging 'bourgeoisie'. Devoting themselves to production and commerce and by the imperialism of the state, the middle classes made the city rich, enabling it to become the primary cultural and artistic centre of Egypt.

The principal and most ancient part of Thebes stretched along the west bank of the Nile, around the great temples of Luxor and Karnak. These temple complexes were

Seated statue of the god Amon with Tutankhamun, c.1330 BC. Musée du Louvre, Paris. From this god was derived one of the names by which Thebes was known.

The Names of Thebes

The ancient name of the city was Uase (Sceptre), although the name No-Amon (City of Amon) was also used. It subsequently became Diospolis Magna, the 'Great City of Jupiter', with whom Amon was identified.

representative of the New Kingdom, in the same way that the Memphite pyramids were representative of the Old Kingdom. On the opposite bank (West Thebes) were erected the sparse suburbs of the workers and free citizens, and beyond these, on the

rocky coastline, the funerary temples and necropolises of the pharaohs and their consorts; the Valley of the Kings and the Valley of the Queens. In this way, the gently flowing Nile separated the world of the living from that of the dead.

Temple of Amon-Ra, showing the first pillar, c.1260 BC. Luxor. This was the entrance to the temple, giving access to a spacious courtyard.

Karnak: the Home of Amon-Ra

The great temple courtyard, c.1260 BC. Temple of Amon-Ra, Karnak. The power and wealth of Thebes in this period are exemplified by the magnificence of its huge temple complexes.

Karnak was a very important mixed religious and residential centre, home to the king of the gods, Amon-Ra, and all the pharaohs from the beginning of the New Kingdom. Nowadays, its ruins cover two hectares. The grand complex, called al-Karnak by the Arabs and Ipe Isut by the ancient Egyptians was developed over the course of 2,000 years.

It was divided into three zones, consecrated to the three members of the triad of Thebes; Amon, his wife, Mut and their son, Khonsu. There were also temples dedicated to other divinities. The temple of Montu, the 'Lord of Thebes', god of war, can be found in the northern part of the complex, while the temple of Mut, Amon's spouse, is in the south. Within the city walls there is the temple of Khonsu, a temple of Ramses III, the temples of Ptah and of Sekhmet, the Celebration Hall of Thutmosis III, a small temple of Amenhotep II, a chapel of Thutmosis III and the temple of Osiris and Opet.

The main constituent parts of the great temple of Amon are the same as those found in other official temples: a central pillar, a courtyard surrounded by a portico, a great hypostyle hall, a vestibule, a sanctuary and a sacristy. Additional pillars, courtyards with portico and sanctuaries were erected by subsequent sovereigns, each of whom wished to enlarge or embellish the temple. Having passed the gigantic principal pillar, you arrive in the great courtyard surrounded by its portico, in which can be found a temple of Ramses III, a sanctuary of Seti I and a granite sphinx of Taharqa. The *bas-reliefs* of the temple are numerous and important, documenting the military campaigns of Seti I and Ramses II in Asia.

View of the Temple of Khonsu, commissioned by Ramses III (1184-1153 BC). Karnak.

Obelisk of Thutmosis I, c.1500 BC. Temple of Amon-Ra, Karnak. Many pharaohs dedicated themselves to the embellishment of the magnificent complex of Karnak, commissioning temples, statues and obelisks.

Luxor: The House of Amon and Mut

Courtyard of Ramses II, Eighth century BC. Luxor. This pharaoh was responsible for the enlargement of the temple founded by Amenhotep III.

The ancient Egyptians called the temple of Luxor 'Ta-ipetresi' (Harem meridionale), which the Greeks understood as Thebes, a name frequently used for the whole zone. Dedicated to the Theban trio of Amon, Mut and Khonsu, it was commissioned towards 1380 BC by Amenhotep III, and a hundred years later Ramses II had it enlarged to its current dimensions of 190m x 55m.

The entrance to the temple consists of a great pillar, on which are engraved scenes from the victories achieved by Ramses II over

the Hittites, and four colossal statues of the pharaoh (two of which depict him seated, the other two standing). Of the two original obelisks, only the one on the eastern side remains; the one to the west was taken away in 1831 and can be seen in the Place de la Concorde in Paris. Through the open courtyard, added by Ramses II, is a pretty colonnade that once provided access to the temple of Amenhotep III. Between the columns stand granite statues of the pharaoh, which were later appropriated by Ramses II. On the interior walls, *bas-reliefs* show the jubilee celebration of Opet, which prompted the building of the temple. The subsequent great courtyard, opened by Amenhotep III and surrounded by columns in the form of papyrus buds, is

The Festival of Opet

Once a year, on the 19th day of the 2nd month of the season of inundation, the statues of Amon and Mut were carried out of the temples in Karnak, placed in the cabin of the ceremonial boat, and carried on the shoulders of the priests along the 1,6-kilometre processional ramp, as far as the temple of Luxor.

Here they would be left for 24 days to celebrate their 'divine honeymoon', during which the conception of their son, Khonsu, took place.

one of the most beautiful in all ancient Egypt. After this is the great hypostyle hall, badly conserved, containing 32 columns. Where the ancient sanctuary once stood, there is now a Christian apse, flanked by two Corinthian columns.

Following pages: Relief showing the procession for the feast-day of Opet, Eighth century BC. Temple of Amon-Ra, Luxor. The temple complex was built to celebrate this annual festival.

THE TEMPLE: HOME TO THE GOD AND TO THE PHARAOH

Model showing the census of livestock, from the tomb of Meketre, Eleventh Dynasty (2055-1650 BC). Egyptian Museum, Cairo. The priests had the task of administering the wealth and property that had been ceded to the temples.

The ceremonial temple was situated at the heart of a group of buildings, and was home to the god and to the pharaohs. Its structure never changed: it was said that the gods themselves had fixed the details, even as far as the height of the walls were concerned.

In the highest and darkest point of every temple was the sanctuary, the place in which the ka (spirit) of the deity resided, being evoked by the statue hidden in the shrine (naos). In theory, only the king could stay in the presence of the god, but in practice he would nominate a delegate (the high priest or first servant of the god), under whose guidance many

other priests and artisans and peasants also operated.

The temples possessed great tracts of land, often exempt from taxation by royal decree, which produced cereals, fruit and vegetables, and provided fodder for the animals destined for the god and food for the personnel assigned to the cult.

Towards 1250 BC, during the reign of Ramses II, more than 80,000 men worked in the temple at Karnak, alongside 400,000 head of livestock. The high priests of Thebes became so powerful that they adopted political roles and managed to make them hereditary. This attempt to establish an independent powerbase led to tension with the monarchy.

Temple of Amon-Ra, showing columns from the great hypostyle entrance hall, c.1260 BC. Karnak. The structure of the temples was rigidly fixed by rules, which were believed to have been dictated by the gods.

Chapel of Thutmosis III, Fifteenth century BC. Luxor. The wealth of the complexes at Luxor and Karnak was matched by the immense power of the priests, who were responsible for its administration.

The Rituals

Only the upper-ranking priests were allowed to approach the statue of the god to whom, three times a day, they brought food and drink. The high priest, or the king if present, would open the bolts on the door to the sanctuary, and enter alone.

Firstly he removed the clothing in which the statue was wrapped and washed it with water and natron. He wiped the delicately painted eyes of the god and dressed it again in clothes of clean linen. Then, reciting the prayers of the ritual, he would evoke the ka, offering it the food and drink for its divine meal. Once the ceremony was over, the doors of the sanctuary were sealed with clay ready for the next day. The high priest would make sure every trace of human presence was eliminated, brushing his own footprints from the sand on the floor.

On the occasion of the most important festivals, the statue would be displayed on a ceremonial wooden boat covered with gold leaf, and carried round the perimeter of the temple walls on the shoulders of the priests, so that the common people could render it homage.

Model of a boat, from the tomb of Tutankhamun, c.1330 BC. Egyptian Museum, Cairo. The model represents the boat used in sacred rituals.

Relief showing scribes, from the Tomb of Horemheb (1323-1295 BC) at Saqqara. Egyptian Museum, Florence. Many scribes were employed in the archives of the temples, where they were kept busy transcribing various different kinds of text.

The Temple School

Opposite: Creation of the new solar disc, c.1140 BC. Tomb of Ramses VI, Valley of the Kings. A large part of the texts and teachings used in the temple schools dealt with mythology and religion.

Papyrus with a medical text, c.1320 BC. British Museum, London.

In every temple complex there was a school or 'house of life'. This was a temple archive, where the copying of religious and didactic texts, narrative compositions, scientific treatises and texts dealing with astronomy and magic took place, in order that they might be studied and preserved. The 'house of life' might be considered a kind of university, in which observations made over the centuries and information gathered by experts would be elaborated and utilised for further investigations.

Medicine (like magic) was strictly linked to religious practices and based on coded rites and formulae. Nevertheless, medical knowledge was extremely advanced, as is demonstrated by the *Papyrus Ebers*, a collection of clinical cases, in which illnesses are described in terms of their symptoms and progression. The heart

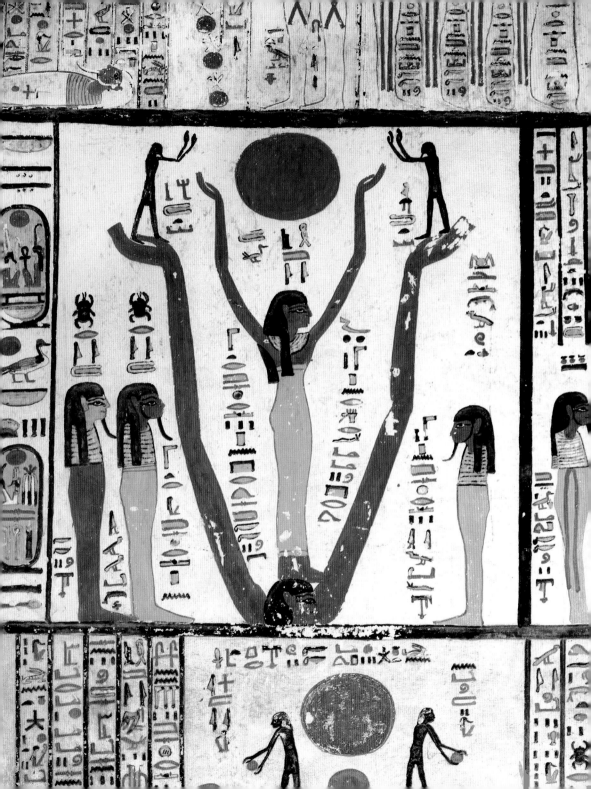

Ostrakon with the *Tale of Sinuhe*, c.1250 BC. British Museum, London. This is one of the most celebrated literary works of ancient Egypt.

was considered to be at the centre of life, its beating linked to the pulse at the wrists.

Surgery was not unknown, especially since the practice of mummification made the Egyptians somewhat expert in human anatomy. Wounds would be closed by cauterisation or with stitches, or by applying a kind of plaster. They even drilled holes in the skull, and made attempts to remove tumours. Anaesthetic was obtained from poppies: the ancient Egyptians knew about opium.

As far a literature was concerned, the schools used 'learned texts', a series of maxims or teachings passed down from ancient times, which outlined correct behaviour. The oldest learned text, found in the library of every temple, was the *Teachings of Ptahhotep*, which went back to the era of the Old Kingdom. This was a sort of practical guide on how to gain success through learning, respect for the hierarchy and moderation. Other examples were the famous *Song of the Harpist*, the *Satire of Trades* and the *Tale of Sinuhe*. During the New Kingdom there also appeared a new type of literature which would nowadays be defined as 'escapist': grotesque and funny stories, war chronicles, and poems of love – which flourished particularly in periods of peace and social order.

Students who wished to study astronomy were less advantaged; the Egyptians never matched the achievements of their neighbours, the Sumerians and Babylonians, in this field, although there would have been exchanges of study and information. Their most important contribution was the subdivision of the day and the night into 12 equal parts, and the solar year into a calendar of 365 days. Observation of the stars also led the Egyptians to distinguish those, which appeared to be mobile (which they called

Papyrus with satirical scenes of animals playing chess, c.1100 BC. British Museum, London.

Papyrus of
*The Book of
the Dead* of
Nedjmet, detail
of the adoration
of the solar
disc, c.1070 BC.
British Museum,
London.

'tireless') from those, which seemed fixed (which they called 'imperishable'). For both they created human and animal figures – a kind of zodiac – linked to mythology and religion.

Then as now, study of theory in these fields was not enough on its own. Aspiring doctors put their knowledge of wounds into practice when accompanying the imperial armies; writers sought out rich patrons whom they could praise and amuse with their compositions. Astronomers got lost in a labyrinth of theories, which they could never demonstrate. For less successful students there was always the possibility of remaining in the temple or sanctuary as scribes or priests; the prestige of these institutions was measured in terms of the number of its adepts.

THE KEY TO THE PAST: SECRETS REVEALED

Napoleon Bonaparte, a General who looked towards the Orient just as Alexander the Great had done; Dominique Vivant Denon, a gentleman, who with a pencil ensured renewed eternity for Egypt; and Jean-François Champollion an enfant prodige, who with determination and imagination unravelled the enigma of hieroglyphics. These are the men who opened up Ancient Egypt to scientific research, and the modern country to European political life.

When Napoleon Bonaparte undertook his campaign in Egypt in 1798, 175 civilian scientists – astronomers and geometers, experts in chemistry and mineralogy, botanists and orientalists, and a considerable number of painters and poets – sailed with the French fleet. They were supplied with a library, which contained nearly all the books about Egypt available at that time in France, and 200 chests with scientific equipment and instruments of measurement.

After the French victory in the Battle of the Pyramids, many of these civilians attached themselves to the troops of General Desaix who, in pursuit of the fleeing Murad-bey (subsequently defeated at Sediman), embarked upon a risky march to Aswan in Upper Egypt. Along the route the scientists and artists measured, made calculations, collected anything that could be carried away and, above all, meticulously drew monuments, colossi, columns, obelisks, hieroglyphics and architectonic particulars.

When Napoleon hastily returned to his homeland, the experts who had reached

Napoleon's Egyptian Campaign

In 1798, Napoleon determined to conquer Egypt, in order to challenge Great Britain in one of its colonial possessions and create a base from which to attack India, one of the sources of British commercial power.

On 19th May, an expedition sailed from Toulon and, after capturing Malta from the Knights, arrived in Alexandria on 1st July. The Mamelukes were defeated near Cairo in the Battle of the Pyramids, but the English admiral, Horatio Nelson, took the French fleet by surprise and destroyed it in the Bay of Abukir, making Napoleon a virtual prisoner.

Upper Egypt continued their frenetic searching, conveying to Cairo all their finds, reproductions, documentation, and animal, vegetable and mineral material, where, in the meantime, the Egyptian Institute had been founded. . The collection contained numerous pieces of earthenware, 27 sculptures – mostly fragments of statues – diverse sarcophagi and some stele (standing stones), including one in black basalt found in Rosetta.

Following defeat at Alexandria, France had to consign all its archaeological booty to Britain. General Hutchinson took care of its transportation, and King George III handed over the precious items to the British Museum.

A whole year of effort and sacrifice on the part of the scientists who accompanied Napoleon to the Nile seemed to have been wasted. However, it subsequently became apparent that the small amount of material that did get to Paris was sufficient to occupy an entire generation of experts, and they had retained all the drawings.

Bronze commemorative medal of the Battle of the Pyramids, 1798. British Museum, London. This was one of the most important battles in Napoleon's Egyptian campaign.

Drawing dating from the Napoleonic expedition in Egypt, showing the portico of the great temple on the island of File.

Versatile Baron:
Dominique Vivant Denon

Amongst the civilians who took part in the Egyptian campaign there was a singular man who had been recommended as an artist to Napoleon by his wife Josephine Beauharnais, queen of the Parisian salons. His name was Dominique Vivant Denon, and at the time he was 51 years old – quite an age at which to go to war for the first time. He had already lived an adventurous life. A baron by birth and a former diplomat, he was stripped of his title and wealth at the outbreak of the revolution, and reduced to selling drawings in order to feed himself, while the heads of many of his friends were falling in the Place de Grève. Fortunately, he gained an unexpected protector in Jacques-Louis David, the painter of the French Revolution, and was able to frequent the salons again, managing to persuade Robespierre to restore his property to him. He came to the attention of the beautiful Josephine, who presented him to Napoleon.

Denon knew nothing about Egypt but was soon under its spell. Close to General Desaix, who respected him like a father, he was tireless during the march towards Aswan, his sketchbook always within reach. He drew the terraced pyramids in Saqqara, the remains of Late Ancient Egypt at Dendera, and the ruins at Thebes. In Elefantina he copied the chapel of Amenhopet III, and his detailed drawing is now the only evidence of the building, which was destroyed in 1822. These drawings subsequently appeared in his autobiography, *Voyage dans l'Haute et Basse Égypte* – which made him rich and famous – and in *Description de l'Égypte*.

On his return to France, he

was appointed director of all its museums and, from 1826, of the Louvre as well. Following in the wake of Napoleon, victorious on so many European battlefields, he gathered a body of works of art, which formed the nucleus of one of France's most important collections.

Detail of the cartouches of Ptolemy and Cleopatra from the *Rosetta Stone*. British Museum, London.

A Name Helps Unravel the Meaning of Hieroglyphics

This drawing shows two cartouches, which appear on both the Rosetta Stone and an obelisk carried to England from the Island of File. Doctor Thomas Young (1773-1829), a genial man who became interested in Egyptology by chance, guessed that the signs represented sounds, not symbols, and that the cartouches contained the names of kings. In 1818, using the Greek part of the stele as a reference point, he deciphered the names of Ptolemy and Cleopatra. The initial letter of the first cartouche was identical to the fifth letter of the second. It was the letter 'p': consequently, the rectangle must correspond to the sound 'p'.

In the same way, the third letter of the first cartouche was identical to the fourth letter of the second cartouche: the letter 'o'. Progressing slowly, he managed to decipher the name P - T - O - L - M - II - S in the first cartouche, and K - L - I - O - P - A - D - R - A in the second. But Young was chiefly a connoisseur of the natural sciences and did not have the philological expertise to do more than decipher a few words.

The Key to Deciphering: the *Rosetta Stone*

In Raschid (Rosetta), in the Nile Delta, on 19th July, 1799, a black basalt stone, about the size of a carriage wheel, was found by chance. It was covered with writing in three sections. On the upper part there were 14 lines of hieroglyphics; in the centre, 22 lines in Demotic Egyptian; and in the bottom section, 54 lines in Greek capital letters. After examining a copy of the three texts, a Swedish diplomat called Akerbald, who was expert in oriental languages, realised that the names of kings in the Greek section appeared in the same position in the Demotic text and hypothesised that the three sections were translations of a single text: the protocol of the sacerdotal college of Memphis, praising Ptolemy V Epiphanes for the subsidy he had agreed to provide for a temple, dated 2nd March, 196 BC. In the Ptolemaic era, when government functions were in the hands of Greeks and Greek was the official language, all public acts were published in two languages, and Greek and Egyptian.

Rosetta Stone, 196 BC. British Museum, London. Texts from the famous trilingual stele enabled the deciphering of hieroglyphics.

Giuseppe Angelelli, *The Franco-Tuscan Expedition to Egypt*. Egyptian Museum, Florence. Among the various people depicted is Champollion, the expert responsible for deciphering hieroglyphics.

Detail of a portrait of Champollion by Giuseppe Angelelli, in his *The Franco-Tuscan Expedition to Egypt*, Egyptian Museum, Florence.

Jean-François Champollion

Jean-François Champollion was born at Figeac in 1790, a child prodigy who studied Arabic, Syrian, Chaldean and Coptic.

In 1801, the famous physicist and mathematician, Jean-Baptiste Fourier (1768-1830), who had taken part in the Egyptian Campaign and become secretary of the Egyptian Institute in Cairo, showed Champollion a copy of the Rosetta Stone. This began the final phase of deciphering the hieroglyphics, concluding in 1822 with the publication of *Lettre à M. Dacier relative a l'alphabet des hiéroglyphes phonétiquese.*

After years studying at his desk, Champollion finally visited Egypt in 1828. It was a triumphant occasion, with people flocking to see the man who 'was able to read the writings of the ancient stones'. He died prematurely four years later.

After 1,500 Years Egyptian Writing Can Be Read Again!

The results of Young's work were sent to Jean-François Champollion in France. It took two years for him to be convinced that the hieroglyphics were not simply symbols but, once he accepted their phonetic nature, he was not only able to rapidly identify the signs, but also to understand the ancient language well enough to make a complete translation of the hieroglyphic section. He did not interpret single words or letters like Young, but instead understood the system behind them.

Champollion wrote the following to the secretary of the Royal French Academy of Inscriptions, Baron Joseph Dacier: 'I have reached the point at which I can have a complete view of the general structure of this form of writing, signs and rules and their combination [...] thus there are the foundations for the grammar book and the dictionary of this writing, which can be found on most monuments'.

Unfortunately Champollion was not to see the publication of his book; he died of a heart attack in 1832. But, after more than 1,500 years, it had become possible for scholars to read ancient Egyptian texts and study a whole new body of information.

Detail of hieroglyphics from a wall painting of Thutmosis III worshipping Amon-Ra, c.1450 BC. Chapel of Hathor, Deir el-Bahari.

Egyptmania

Egyptmania has appeared in a variety of guises – sometimes genuine, sometimes kitsch: the influence of ancient Egypt's decorative arts ranging from music to architecture, furnishings to jewellery, the theatre to make-up.

From the end of the 1700s, ornaments in the form of obelisks, sphinxes and pyramids began to decorate the houses of the bourgeois. The Imperial style of the Napoleonic period came to an end and art nouveau enthusiastically used the archaeological discoveries from ancient Egypt in order to create furniture, jewellery and costumes, and as the inspiration for ballets. The architect and engraver, Giambattista Piranesi (1720–78), became famous for his improbable 'Egyptian' interior designs. A century later the librettist, Camille Du Locle, used a short story by Auguste Mariette as the basis for *Aida*, which was set to music by Giuseppe

Drawing by Giambattista Piranesi for the wall decoration of the Caffè degli Inglesi in Piazza di Spagna, Rome, 1769. British Library, London. Piranesi produced many engravings inspired by ancient Egyptian art.

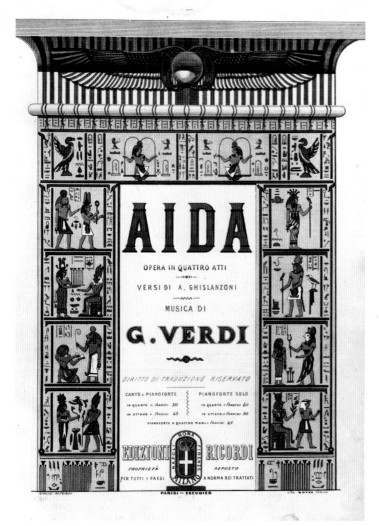

Verdi and performed for the first time in Cairo in 1871.

The taste for things Egyptian has also influenced literature: Thomas Mann's *Joseph and his Brothers,* Christian Jacq's *The Cycle of Ramses II,* Finn Mika Waltari's *Sinuhe the Egyptian.* But, in the Twentieth century, it was cinema, which exploited ancient Egypt most assiduously, with *The Ten Commandments, Cleopatra,* and *The Mummy.* Meanwhile, on television, the mysteries of the Sphinx of Giza, mummies and pyramids are frequent topics. In the world of recent music, there is Philip Glass's *Akhnaten.*

The vocal score of *Aida* by Giuseppe Verdi, title page, 1872. Pierpont Morgan Library, New York,

Charlton Heston and Katherine Cornell act in *Anthony and Cleopatra* on Broadway in 1947. The cinema was also influenced by the glamour of ancient Egypt. Leonia Celli Collection, Rome.

EGYPT TODAY

As we come to the end of our survey of the pharaohs of the Eighteenth Dynasty and the splendours of the New Kingdom, let us bring things to a conclusion by returning to Tutankhamun, the youthful pharaoh brought to light by Carter and Carnarvon, with all his rich 'cortège', which can now be admired in the Egyptian Museum in Cairo.

Let us leave behind the story of the great military successes of the pharaohs and of their efficient social organization, which they were able to maintain for centuries.

Let us also leave behind the description of the magnificent ruins of Luxor and Karnak and of life as it was lived there, and return to our time, inside the arid and fascinating Valley of the Kings.

A Brief Tour of the Valley of the Kings

The tomb of Tutankhamun can be found almost at the centre of the necropolis, just a few metres away from the huge tomb of Ramses VI. There are numerous tombs nearby, all richly decorated, although not many are open to the public. Some – such as that of Ramses II – have partially sunk into the sand.

Particularly interesting is the splendid tomb of Seti I, discovered by Giovanni Battista Belzoni in 1817, where several representations of the pharaoh in front of the goddess Hathor were found. This is the largest and deepest tomb, consisting of a long series of halls and corridors, the walls of which are richly decorated. Some paintings are incomplete, due to the sudden death of the pharaoh, and display signs of having been corrected. Of a simpler construction, but also elaborately decorated, with divinities and scenes from the underworld, are the tombs of Thutmosis III and Amenhotep II. On a secondary branch of the necropolis can be found some smaller tombs. At the beginning of the last century, the tombs of Yuya and Tuyu – the in-laws of Amenhotep III – were discovered in this area, with both mummies still intact. The precious objects, which accompanied them, are now on display in the Egyptian Museum.

Relief of Seti I and the goddess Hathor, c.1280 BC. Egyptian Museum, Florence. This relief comes from the tomb of pharaoh Seti I, discovered in the Valley of the Kings.

Moving on to the Valley of the Queens

Alongside the Valley of the Kings is the Valley of the Queens, designed for the burials of the queens and princesses of the Nineteenth and Tweitieth Dynasties. After this era the Valley was abandoned, and the only finds from a later period are the burial places of some priestesses of the Tenth century BC. Their tunnels, dug into the rocky walls, were subsequently used by Christian hermits at the beginning of modern times. There are about 80 tombs in the Valley of the Queens, not all of them completed, whilst others have greatly deteriorated. The most famous is that of Nefertari, which contains paintings of the queen in front of the divinity, and playing chess.

Picture of the queen playing chess, Eighth century BC. Tomb of Queen Nefertari, Thebes.

The picture is located in the best known of the tombs in the Valley of the Queens.

CHANGES TO THE NILE

The northern
basin of the
Aswan Dam, in
a photograph
taken on
10th October,
1912. National
Museum of
Science and
Industry,
London.

The Nile has altered
enormously, not only since
the time of Tutankhamun,
but even since that of
Carter and Mariette.

The transformation of its
flow began in the first decades
of the 1800s, when the

reforming Viceroy Mohamed
Ali, with the aid of the Piedmont
Bernardino Drovetti (1776-
1852), General Consol for
France in Egypt, set to work on
a project that ended in 1890.

The continuous flow of
the Nile was transformed

into a system of basins contained by dams.

A first great dam was constructed to the north of Cairo (the so-called *Barrage du Nil*), and other smaller dams were built at Assiut, Nang Hammadi and Esna, whilst a fifth, at Aswan, went up in several stages. These dams replaced the seasonal inundations with an artificial system, which allowed for the uninterrupted cultivation of the land. This produced two or three harvests per year but impeded the deposits of silt and the renewal of the soil, making fertilisers necessary.

Between 1934 and 1950, the population of Egypt doubled to about 28 million, and the narrow strip of fertile land on the two banks of the Nile became insufficient to feed everyone. The decision was made in the 1950s to construct

Glass container in the shape of a fish, from Tel el-Amarna, c.1350 BC. British Museum, London. Many works of art were inspired by Egypt's natural environment and by its fauna.

The northern basin of the Aswan Dam in a photograph taken on 23rd December, 1912. London, National Museum of Science and Industry.

a great dam at Sadd el-Aali, behind the Aswan dam.

Work began in 1960 and was concluded eleven years later. The dam is 980 metres thick at its base, 3.6 kilometres wide and 109 metres above the original level of the Nile. The quantity of building material used in its construction was 17 times greater than that required for the Great Pyramid of Cheops at Giza.

The dam at Sadd el-Aali represents one of the most significant changes to the face of the earth carried out by mankind. It provides electrical energy for industry, and water to irrigate the reclaimed land.

However, upriver, two thirds of the cultivatable land of Nubia has been submerged as far as the Third Cataract.

It is covered by Lake Nasser, which is 500 kilometres long, 9.6 kilometres wide and 182 metres deep.

CONTEMPORARY TUTANKHAMUN

Even though the discovery of the tomb of Tutankhamun goes back many decades, research continues on his mummy and on the objects, which accompanied him.

Tutankhamun has undergone ever newer investigations over the years – from the X-raying of his corpse in order to discover what illness or accident caused his death, to the close examination of his headgear, tunics, sandals, kilts and other garments.

The restoration of the tomb, which currently welcomes an average of 3,000 visitors a day, also continues to offer a challenge. In order to conserve its wall paintings, an Italian team, which had used avant-garde techniques on the tomb of Nefertari, was consulted.

The precious objects from the tomb, one of the major attractions at the Egyptian Museum, still bring in huge numbers of visitors, and the exhibition of these artefacts outside Egypt – for example, Basle in 2004 – is always a significant event. More than 80 years after the discovery of his tomb, the general public's interest in Tutankhamun is as potent as ever.

Container for the internal organs of Tutankhamun, from the tomb of the pharaoh, c.1330 BC. Egyptian Museum, Cairo. The precious funeral treasure of Tutankhamun is one of the most important collections in the museum.

Divinities
rejoicing,
c.1295 BC.
Valley of
the Kings,
Tomb of
Ramses I.